Parties for Children

Also by Jean Marzollo

Supertot: A Parent's Guide to Toddlers
Illustrated by Irene Trivas (Unwin Paperbacks)

by Jean Marzollo and Janice Lloyd

Learning Through Play
Illustrated by Irene Trivas (Unwin Paperbacks)

PARTIES FOR CHILDREN

How to Give Them, How to Survive Them

By JEAN MARZOLLO
Illustrated by IRENE TRIVAS

London
UNWIN PAPERBACKS
Boston   Sydney

First published in Great Britain by Unwin Paperbacks 1984
Reprinted 1984, 1985

UNWIN® PAPERBACKS
40 Museum Street, London, WC1A 1LU, UK

Unwin Paperbacks
Park Lane, Hemel Hempstead, Herts, HP2 4TE, UK

George Allen & Unwin Australia Pty Ltd,
8 Napier Street, North Sydney, NSW 2060, Australia

Copyright© 1983 Jean Marzollo and Irene Trivas.
First published in the USA by Harper & Row Publishers Inc.
British publication rights arranged with Sheldon Fogelman.

British Library Cataloguing in Publication Data

Marzollo, Jean
  [Birthday parties for children] Parties
for children: how to give them, how to
survive them.
1. Children's parties   2. Birthdays
I. Title   II. Parties for children: how
to give them, how to survive them
793.2′1   GV1205
ISBN 0–04–793065–9

Printed in Great Britain by
Guernsey Press Co. Ltd, Guernsey, Channel Islands

With special thanks to Geraldine Van Dusen, who suggested the book, and to her children, Norah and Caitlin, who inspired her suggestion.

Thanks also to Sheilah Gross, Katy Taylor, Dorothy McHutchison, and Sheila Rauch for their ideas.

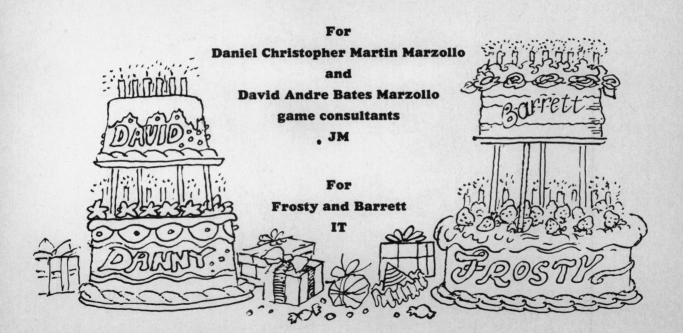

For
Daniel Christopher Martin Marzollo
and
David Andre Bates Marzollo
game consultants
. JM

For
Frosty and Barrett
IT

Contents

Introduction

Melissa is two years old. It is her birthday party. She is all dressed up in a pink dress, white tights, and new blue shoes. Her room, decorated with twisted streamers of pink crepe paper, is filled with ten two-year-olds from her playgroup. Melissa's mother is serving a drink to the ten mothers, who are chatting happily in the living room. The children are wandering, actually waddling (most of them are still in nappies), gleefully around the room, touching things and playing with Melissa's new toys. Where is Melissa? She is in her cot crying. She has never seen so much confusion. Her mother keeps saying to the other mothers, with a frantic laugh, "I don't know what's the matter with her." Everyone is having a good time, it appears, except Melissa and her mother.

David is five. It is his birthday party. Last year at this time, Danny—his older brother by two years—ruined the party by winning all the games. This year Danny and David have made a deal: Danny will not participate in any of the games; instead, he will announce them. I, their mother, feel this is a brilliant solution to the chaos sibling rivalry can cause at a birthday party. So, the time comes for the games. Danny announces a beanbag toss, and one by one the guests take turns. Scores are tallied, and Danny announces that Jed has won, whereupon David bursts into tears. He is sobbing inconsolably. Finally, *finally*, when he calms down, he tells me he thought that since his *brother* was running the games, he was going to *win* them all, just as his brother had last year. What a party that was going to be! How he was looking forward to it! We go on with the party somehow, but David never quite recovers from his disillusionment.

What Makes a Birthday Child Cry

1. Too much anticipation ahead of time
2. Too much confusion at the party
3. Too much attention focused on someone else (sibling, guest clown, or magician)
4. Too many other children sharing toys (put special toys away ahead of time)
5. Too many misconceptions (that the birthday child will win every game; that everyone will do what he or she wants; that the birthday child will get all the attention)

Matt is eight. His mother drops him off at a classmate's house for a birthday party. A few hours later Matt is delivered home, whereupon he tells about the violent murder movie to which he and the other children at the party were "treated." Matt's mother is furious. She had no idea he was going to this movie. If she had known, she would have kept Matt at home.

What kind of a mother would take a bunch of eight-year-olds to a murder movie? A mother who has held children's birthday parties in her home before and, frazzled after the last one, declares, "Never again"; a mother who works and has no time to plan something for her child; a mother who, like Matt's friend's, does not know what to do so decides, "I'll take them to Cinema 4 on Saturday afternoon. Something will be playing." Something is playing. It is a murder movie. "Oh, well," she says, "at least they'll like the popcorn and soda, and they'll be quiet. And then it will all be over for another year."

As of this writing I have given fourteen birthday parties for my two children. None was so terific I want to brag about it. Several went fine. Once a child had to be taken to the emergency room because she had cut her hand on a metal frog-clicker toy. Many, many times it rained. Every time there were at least some tears. Still, each year, my children can't wait for their parties. I have never heard them say, "I don't ever, ever want to have another birthday party." It is only I and my friends who say that and who approach party day with dread.

The problem is, I guess, that we expect too much. We want this year's party to be better than last year's. We want to make our children happy on

Recipe for a Successful Birthday Party

1. Be specific about when the party starts and *ends*.
2. Keep it small.
3. Keep it short.
4. Play age-appropriate games.
5. Have only one or two special events.
6. Have a cooling-off activity for afterwards.
7. Plan ahead, but expect the unexpected.

this special day. We love our children and want to express this love with a special, wonderful celebration. We want our children to have fun at the stroke of the clock, to feel overjoyed, and to express bliss graciously from two to four P.M. Every year we want this even though we know that it's a little much to ask anyone to experience two straight hours of ecstasy, and it's very unrealistic for us to think that we can ever make that happen.

The question is, then, What can we *realistically* expect to happen at a child's birthday party?

We can realistically expect a special feeling in the air. This feeling need not be one of frenzy; it can be quietly anticipatory.

We can realistically expect that the birthday child will happily open presents, but may not express appreciation for each one. We will probably have to remind the little darling to say thanks.

We can realistically expect that what the birthday child will like best about the party will be not the money we have spent or the time we put into making homemade party baskets, but rather the friends that are gathered together (when else do we invite that many children over all at once?) and the help we give everyone playing games (when else do we ever do that?).

When the party is over, we can realistically expect that the birthday child will feel let down and we will feel dazed, if not a little traumatized. This is a good time for a cooling-off activity. Perhaps we can plan to sit down with the birthday child and look over the new presents, play a game, or read a book together. We might even want to save one of our presents to give to the child at this time. Another good idea is to invite one guest to stay later than the others so that the sudden departure of friends is not so abrupt and total.

It seems to me that the most successful birthday parties are often the least elaborate. They follow the basic steps in the ritual: invitations, decorations, presents, desserts of cake and ice cream, games, treat bags for everyone, goodbyes, and it's over. The ritual need not be jazzed up, but if it is, only one or two special things are added. The cake may be unusual, the decorations may be out of the ordinary, one game may be a cleverly worked-out treasure hunt, but basically the party follows the plan the children expect. Too many special things are just that: too much. For the best time, keep the party simple.

The best parties are short. An hour is perfect for toddlers. An hour and a half is fine for children four to six. Two hours might be okay for children seven to ten, especially if they are playing a game, such as rounders or football, but an hour and a half is still fine. Better to stop a party short than let it disintegrate.

If you can, keep the party small. You've probably heard the advice to invite only as many children as the age of the child: one guest for a one-year-old, two guests for a two-year-old, and so on. This is a brilliant concept that I'm sure would contribute to party success, but I have never seen anyone follow it. Either we want more children to contribute to the party mood, or we want more children to bring our child gifts, or our child has

too many friends and wants to invite them all. But try. Try hard to keep the party as small as possible.

I think the hardest part for a parent giving a birthday party is running the games. It's relatively easy to send out invitations, to make or buy a cake, and to set a party table. But how do you know ahead of time which games to play? If you pick games that are too easy for the children, they won't like them. If you pick games that are too hard, they will cry in frustration. If you pick games that are unfamiliar and complicated, you'll end up yelling in a shrill voice and getting a headache. (A birthday party headache, with its distinct sensation of pain at the temples and a whirlwind around you, is to be avoided at all costs.) If you pick noisy, rambunctious games and it rains, you are sure to get one of these headaches. If you pick games that are too short, you will end up looking at your watch in despair, realizing there's another hour to go for which you have no plans. If you let the children run all over the house, they'll probably like it. How bad can that be? Pretty bad. Knowing a little more about children's games can prevent such torture.

I hope the ideas in this book will give you enough to go by so that when you close the door after the last guest leaves at the next birthday party, you'll feel that what has just ended was not a nightmare but a celebration.

Good luck.

How to Have a Low-Cost Party

1. Call the children to invite them, or make your own invitations. Your child can decorate paper or index cards with drawings, make prints of onions or other vegetables with paint or a stamp pad, or use stickers. Your child can write the information about the party too, if he or she is old enough.

2. Ask the children to design and colour their own tablecloth or mats. Tape white shelf paper on the table or spread newspapers—black-and-white funnies, for example—and provide crayons. Use round coffee filters for place mats and provide marking pens.

3. Serve only cake (make it if you can), ice cream, and juice.

4. Play noncompetitive games so that you don't have to buy any prizes to give out. Don't feel cheap about this. Children are often happier playing noncompetitive games. Or put a gold sticker on everyone's nose who wins a game, or give the winners special armbands.

5. Don't give out treat bags and bags of sweets. At the end of the party give every child a paper-bag mask or a bag of crisps. Or make some special projects as favours (see Chapter 4). 4).

6. Don't feel guilty about economizing. The children will have just as much fun as if you had spent lots of money. The best things in life (and at birthday parties) really are free: love and friendship.

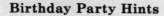

Birthday Party Hints

1. Have your child, if over the age of four, help you plan the party. This way your child will know what is happening and will be less apt to have unrealistic expectations.

2. Tie balloons outside your door so guests will know where you live.

3. Serve food and drinks children like. Don't get fancy. If you are worried about spills, serve lemonade. It doesn't stain rugs.

4. Choose games the children know how to play. Ask your child or your child's teacher which games are favourites.

5. Make sure the first person It in games is the birthday party child.

6. Remember that not all the children have to play all the games. Some children prefer to watch or play with toys. That's okay. Don't be a tyrant.

7. Don't just give out treat bags. Make the children hunt for them. It is more fun that way, and it takes up more time.

8. Have the party at the park or playground for a change. Tell everyone what time to meet and where. Serve food there and let the children play as they always do. At the end, give everyone a bag of crisps or a balloon. Easy!

9. Be ready for parents coming to pick up their children on time. Have the last game end with putting on coats or getting treat bags.

10. If you like, send thank-you notes to each child at the party. Make a list when presents are being opened or ask another grownup to keep track.

How to Use This Book to Plan a Party

1. Read the book all the way through. Make notes of the ideas you like best.

2. Decide what kind of party you want.

3. Go back and read the suggestions for that party.

4. Keep in mind that everything you read is only a suggestion. Discard suggestions that are too old or too young for the age group of the children you're inviting. Discard suggestions you don't care for. Keep in mind that most inside games can be played outside, but only some of the outside games can be played inside. Many games can be played either competitively or noncompetitively.

5. Decide what food to serve. The food suggestions for each party are intended to start you thinking. There are lots of other ideas in the chapter on food.

6. Combine your notes. Make a party plan. If necessary, make two plans: a good-weather plan and a rainy-day plan. If you don't have enough ideas, go through the whole book again to find more.

7. Share the plan with your child so he or she can contribute ideas and know what's going to happen. If you're a child planning a party, go over your plans thoroughly with your parents.

8. Begin preparations once your plan is firm.

9. Be sure you have everything you need before the party starts. Keep your plan handy for reference.

10. Remember that nothing ever goes exactly as planned.

HAPPY BIRTHDAY

HAPPY BIRTHDAY

3

Chapter 1

Parties for Children 1–3

Toddler parties should be very small. Five children should be the maximum. Often it's pleasant to have parents and older relatives. They bring presents and contribute to the festive spirit, yet don't have to be entertained. You do have to serve them, though, and sometimes this duty can distract you from the children. Ask another parent or relative to take over that function so you won't have to think about it.

One hour is long enough. You don't need to bother to decorate or plan special games. Often it's enough to put out some toys for the children to share. Ask your toddler ahead of time, "Are there any toys you don't want to share?" Put them away.

Keep the agenda flexible. Open presents, serve cupcakes and ice cream, take pictures, and let the toddlers play. Skip hard sweets and nuts: small children can choke on them. Skip balloons. Children can put popped ones in their mouths and choke on them, too.

Children this age may enjoy being read to. Select a book with big pictures everyone can see. Ask the local children's librarian to help you. Tell her the age of the children coming to the party. Often it helps to read to the children (or play a record for them) while they're eating.

You can be so relaxed about a party for a one- and two-year-old that you need not even have one. At supper some evening put a candle on a cupcake and have fun helping your child blow it out. At this age no more hoopla is needed.

But in case you feel the urge to have a real party, the ideas in this chapter may help.

Party for a child turning 1

Menu

Hard, teething-type biscuits
Unfrosted cupcakes (frosted ones are too messy)
Ice cream
Milk or juice
Food and beverages for the grownups

Decorations

If possible, use or set up a very low table so that the
children can sit comfortably and safely. Use low
chairs or boxes.
Ask each child to bring his or her bottle or drinking
cup.
Skip paper tablecloths and napkins. The children could
rip them and eat them.
Baby-proof the house for the party. (Put away break-
able and dangerous objects.)

Favours

Teething biscuits, teething toys, squeak toys that
can't be chewed open, plastic keys on a chain, tennis
balls, rattles, bath toys, measuring spoons.

Plan

1. Greet the children and their parents.
2. Bring each child to the play area.
3. Help the birthday child open the presents.
4. Serve the children food at a low table. Ask a friend to serve the grownups.
5. Take photographs.
6. Try reading the children picture books while they are seated. Some good ones for this age group are *Each Peach Pear Plum* by Janet and Allan Ahlberg and *One Hunter* by Pat Hutchins. Read them over again if the children seem interested. If they are seated low and comfortably, the children may be content to sit and stare for a surprisingly long time. If a child goes off to play, don't worry about it as long as the child is supervised and safe.
7. Play Pat-a-Cake, Pat-a-Cake.
8. Let the children play again in the play area.
9. Give the children their favours on the way out.

Park Party

Instead of having the party inside a house, invite the children and their parents to the park. Meet at a certain time and place. Or just bring birthday goodies to the park and celebrate with whoever is there.

Party for a child turning 2

Menu

Cupcakes (served first)
Ice cream cones (served after the cupcakes are eaten)
Milk or juice
Food and beverages for the grownups

Decorations

Use a low table, or put a tablecloth on the floor and sit
around it.
Fancy decorations are unnecessary for this age. If anything, just buy a tablecloth with pictures children
like.
Regarding balloons, make sure the children don't put
pieces of popped ones in their mouths to chew. They
can choke on such pieces. It might be better to skip
balloons until the children are older.

Favours, Items for Treat Bags

Bell bracelets (securely sew bells on bracelets made
from elastic), toy horns, little plastic wrist watches,
paint-with-water books.

Plan

1. Greet the children and their parents.
2. Bring each child to the play area.
3. Help the birthday child open the presents.
4. Serve the children food. Ask a friend to serve the grownups.
5. Take photographs.
6. Read to the children while they are eating. Try *The Very Hungry Caterpillar* by Eric Carle, *Mister Magnolia* by Quentin Blake and *The Troublesome Pig* by Priscilla Lamont.
7. Sing songs that the children know. "Row, Row, Row Your Boat"; "Jingle Bells"; "Twinkle, Twinkle, Little Star" are familiar ones.
8. Do finger-play games the children know, such as Itsy Bitsy Spider.
9. Play Ring-a-ring-a-Roses.
10. Play Follow the Leader.
11. Let the children play some more.
12. Give the children their favours on the way out.

9

Party for a child turning 3

Menu

Cupcakes (served first)
Ice cream cones (served after the cupcakes)
Milk or juice (small cans of apple juice are convenient)
Food and beverages for those grownups who wish to
stay at the party

Decorations

Cover the table with newspaper and let the children
scribble all over it with crayons.
Make newspaper party hats.

Favours, Items for Treat Bags

Bananas, animal biscuits, apples, party hats, toy
horns, toy cars, plastic figures (of firemen, soldiers,
cowboys, Indians, dinosaurs), small dolls, ribbons,
crayons.

I AM THREE
AND THERE'S A PARTY FOR
ME!

NAME _____
PLACE _____
DATE _____
FROM _____ TO _____
RSVP
P.S. PARENTS WELCOME.

Plan

1. Greet the children and their parents.
2. Bring each child to the play area.
3. Help the birthday child open the presents.
4. Serve the children food. Ask a friend to serve the grownups.
5. Take photographs.
6. Read to the children while they are eating. Try *Ask Mr. Bear* by Marjorie Flack, *In the Night Kitchen* by Maurice Sendak, and *The Little Engine That Could* by Watty Piper.
7. Ask the children what songs they'd like to sing.
8. Ask them if they know any finger-play games. Do them.
9. Play musical-action games, such as Ring-a-Ring-a-Roses, London Bridge, and Hokey Pokey.
10. Sit in a circle. Spread legs so that everyone's feet touch. Roll a ball back and forth to each other. Try this to music.
11. Let the children play some more.
12. Give the children toy horns and have a parade.
13. Turn the parade into Follow the Leader with the birthday child as the leader. Then let a grownup be the leader and lead everyone to their coats or a place where favours are given out.
14. The party is over.

NEWSPAPER PARTY HATS
Here's how to make them:

1.

2. FOLD

3.

4. FOLD UP · TAPE

Chapter 2

Parties for Children 4–10

On the following pages you will find ideas for many parties. Both parents and children can look at these pages. Younger children can see from the pictures which parties excite them. Older children can read through the recommendations and plan their parties themselves, with parents needed only to approve final plans. In other words, this is a section for parents and children to share. Once a certain party has been decided on, don't feel you have to follow the recommendations exactly. There may be ideas suggested for other parties that you want to incorporate into your party. Fine.

The game suggestions are only suggestions. Instructions for playing most of the games mentioned here or making things will be found in the chapters on games and projects. Read through those chapters and pick the ones you would most like to play or do. Change the titles of games to fit the theme of your party. For example, instead of Pin the Tail on the Donkey, you might play Pin the Fangs on Dracula or Pin the Horn on the Unicorn: find or make a picture and tape it to the refrigerator or wall. Cut out fangs or horns or whatever from construction paper. Use tape or one of the plastic sticky gums (such as Blue Tak) available at hardware departments, instead of pins.

The foods listed under the menus are also just suggestions. The recipes will be found in the chapter on food.

For a change of pace, try giving one of these parties in the early evening, serving a light dinner meal and passing out torches for favours. For many children it is a special treat to play games in the semidark. Be sure the children are old enough and well supervised. You might also try a breakfast party.

Apples and autumn leaves party

Menu

Apple pie
Vanilla ice cream
Apple juice

OPTIONAL:
Toffee apples

Decorations

Ask the birthday child to collect autumn leaves
before the party and arrange them in a design all
over the top of a plain paper tablecloth. Tape the
leaves in place.
Use a vase of autumn branches for a centrepiece.
Use autumn colours for plates, napkins, and cups.
Set an apple on each plate. Print each child's name on
a piece of masking tape and tape it to the apple.

Favours, Prizes, Items for Treat Bags

Fresh apples, bags of nuts, toffee apples, small cans
of apple juice.

Note: Since this party comes in the autumn, you may wish
to combine it with a Halloween Party.

Inside Games and Activities, Competitive and Noncompetitive

1. Bob for Apples. Fill a tub with water and float apples in it, one for each child. To play, the children kneel, put their hands behind their backs, and try to pick up an apple with their teeth. Young children need help.

2. Tape a Leaf on the Top of a Tree. Play like Pin the Tail on the Donkey. Draw a tree on a big piece of paper and use real leaves. The children can collect them at the party. For younger children, play this game noncompetitively. For example, ask them to pin their leaves anywhere on the tree. It's fun to see where the leaves land.

3. Hot Apple. Play like Hot Potato.

Outside Activities, Noncompetitive

1. Rake leaves into a pile and jump in them.

2. Make a scarecrow stuffed with leaves. Fill a grocery bag with leaves for the head and tie shut. Draw a face with markers. Add an old hat. Stuff an old shirt and trousers with leaves, tying the sleeves, legs, and waist shut. Tie the head, shirt, and trousers together and hang the scarecrow from a tree or prop it up in a dramatic place.

Outside Games, Competitive

1. Leaf Scavenger Hunt. Play like a Scavenger Hunt.

2. Leaf Hunt. Play like a Peanut Hunt. How many leaves can you put in a bag in one minute?

15

Arts and crafts party

Menu

Decorate-Your-Own Cupcakes. Provide bowls of vari-
ously tinted icings, small dishes of hundreds and
thousands and small spreading knives. Older
children can try writing their names on the cupcakes. See Decorator's Icing (page 145).

Ice cream

Tinted milk. Let each child put a few drops of food
colouring in his or her cup (clear plastic cups are
best for this). Let the children experiment to make
different colours: orange from red and yellow, green
from blue and yellow, and so on.

Decorations

Cover the table with newspaper and place bowls of
icing in the centre.

Favours, Prizes, Items for Treat Bags

Crayons, nontoxic markers, paint sets, stickers, pipe
cleaners, paper, tape, paste, clay

BRUSH UP!

Attention:
   All Artists
Come to an Arts and
Crafts Birthday
   Party

For _____
Date _____
From _____ To _____
Place _____
RSVP. Phone _____

Inside Activities, Noncompetitive

1. Make a mural together for the birthday child. Roll white shelf paper out on the floor. Each child decorates a section of it and signs his or her name and the date. Display when the mural is finished.

2. Make decorations and decorate the party room *at the party*.

3. If art supplies are favours, let the children open them up and use them at the party.

4. Art Contest. Have everyone draw a picture. Award everyone a prize for being distinct in a certain way: most realistic, most abstract, best design, funniest, prettiest, weirdest, scariest, most interesting, and so on.

Outside Games and Activities, Noncompetitive

1. Find rocks and paint them with acrylic paints to make paperweights.

2. Treasure Hunt. At the end of the hunt, the treasure box contains art supplies for everyone to share and use at the party.

Outside Games, Competitive

Draw-a-Face Relay Race. Each team member has to run to a chair or line, pick up a pad, draw a face, sign his or her name, drop the pad on the chair or line, and run back to tap the next player on his or her team to go. Each player draws on a different page. The first team to finish wins.

Football party

Menu

Hot dogs or sandwiches
Popcorn
Carrot sticks
Ice cream cones
Cupcakes
Lemonade

Decorations

Use the sports pages from a newspaper as a tablecloth.
For an outdoor picnic, sit on the sidelines of a real
football field where you can go to play or watch a
game.

Favours, Prizes, Items for Treat Bags

Football cards, footballs, football socks, rosettes and
photographs of football players.

Note: A fine birthday party for older children is to take them
to a football pitch and watch a real game. Children should be
nine or older. Younger children get fidgety.

Inside Games and Activities, Noncompetitive

1. Draw-Your-Own Football Team. Give each child
index cards and markers. Have the children draw
themselves and the others at the party as footballers.
Afterwards, give each child the pictures drawn of him
or her as a member of the team.
2. Miss, Miss, Goal. Play like Duck, Duck, Goose.

FOOTBALL BIRTHDAY PARTY

FOR
DATE
FROM TO
PLACE

Inside Games, Competitive

1. Who Am I? Use names of football players.
2. Guess Who They Are. Pin photographs of famous football players around the house and ask the children to write down the names of the players on a piece of paper. Children can work in pairs, if they prefer.
3. Hot Football. Play like Hot Potato.
4. Football Race. Divide the children into two teams and ask them to run from the start-line to the finish-line, one by one, with the football held between their knees, before passing the ball to the next child in the team. The team that finishes first is the winner.

Outside Game and Activity

Play a real football game in the garden or at a local field. For children under eight, invite other grownups or older children to help the game move along. A grownup can be the referee. Invite enough children to field two teams. Ask their parents to leave them and pick them up at the site of the game.

Beach party

Menu

Sandwiches
Cupcakes
Ice cream (purchased at an ice cream stand)
Cans of juice with tab openers

Bring supplies to the beach in a cooler bag.
Don't forget birthday candles and matches.

Decorations

Ask everyone to spread out towels near each other.
Don't bother with fancy party supplies. Just serve the
food as simply as possible. Give each child money for
the ice cream man.

Favours, Prizes, Items for Treat Bags

Balls, Frisbies, playing cards, kites, buckets and
spades

Inside Games (in Case of Rain), Noncompetitive

1. Fish for Presents
2. Peanut Hunt

Bring your own towel and meet on the beach for a Birthday lunch for:

_____

Place _____

Date _____

From _____ To _____

RSVP. Phone _____

(or) If it rains, come to my house _____

Inside Games, Competitive

1. Camouflage
2. Hot Frisbie. Play like Hot Potato.
3. Beach-Ball Toss. Play like Bull's-Eye Toss.
4. Drop the Clothespegs in the Bottle

Outside Activities, Noncompetitive

1. Swimming
2. Collecting shells
3. Building sand castles. Give awards to everyone for his or her castle's particular distinction: prettiest, biggest, smallest, fanciest, simplest, the one you'd most like to live in, and so on.

Outside Games, Competitive

Beach Scavenger Hunt. Play like a Scavenger Hunt. Listed items to find might be a mussel shell, a pink shell, a gold shell, seaweed, driftwood, a piece of rubbish, a piece of smooth sea glass, a feather, and so on. Tell the children where they can go to look for things.

Big party for a whole class

Menu

Hot dogs. Cook them ahead of time, place in rolls, and
keep them warm in the oven, covered with foil.
Potato crisps. Put some on each plate ahead of time.
Juice. Pour it into the cups ahead of time, not too full.
Put candles in the birthday child's cupcake.
Ice Cream Cupcakes (page 148).

Decorations and Serving Procedures

If the table isn't large enough, put a big paper tablecloth on the floor and have the children sit around it.
As soon as the children sit down, they can start on their
crisps and juice. Then serve the hot dogs. To entertain
the children while they eat, read to them, play a record, ask quiz-game questions, such as "What movie is
Sleepy in?" or take turns telling jokes and riddles.

Favours, Prizes, Items for Treat Bags

Sweets, peanuts, apples, balloons, crayons, pencils,
pencil sharpeners

HEAR YE!
HEAR YE!
COME ONE AND ALL!
(OUR WHOLE CLASS IS COMING)
TO MY BIG BIRTHDAY PARTY
NAME _____
PLACE _____
DATE _____
TIME: FROM _____ TO _____
RSVP _____

Inside Games, Noncompetitive

1. Seven-Up
2. Simon Says
3. Sneaky Pete
4. How Long Is a Minute?
5. Hunt for the Ticking Clock. Hide a clock or a cooking timer. Everyone listens and tries to find it. The person who finds it first gets to hide it again.

Inside Games, Competitive

1. Camouflage
2. Peanut Hunt
3. Hot Potato
4. Bull's-Eye Toss
5. How Long Is a Minute?

Outside Games, Noncompetitive

1. Everyone's It
2. The Blob
3. Duck, Duck, Goose
4. Freeze Tag

Outside Games, Competitive

1. Dodge Ball, Rounders, Football
2. Stone
3. Red Rover
4. Relay Races

I have never had a party for a whole class, but my friend Katie Taylor has them four times a year for her four children. Her advice is: "Have the party on a Saturday so your spouse or friends can help. Invite the kids for lunch. That may sound like more work, but it isn't because the children spend extra time eating, and while they're eating, they're quiet. Ahead of time, set the table and put lots of balloons in the party room or garden so that the kids can play with them as soon as they arrive. Open presents while the kids are playing. Serve lunch. Then play games, show cartoons on a movie projector, and if it's feasible, go outside for games. The last game should be a Sweet Hunt or Peanut Hunt. Have extra sweets or peanuts to drop near the kids who aren't finding any. Time the hunt to end as parents arrive. For kids ten and up, send them on a Scavenger Hunt. Hope for good weather. Maximum length for the party, an hour and a half."

Bubbles and balloons party

Menu

Balloon Cake. Tape the strings of as many balloons as
your child's age to the sides of the cake plate. Place
the candles in the center of the cake. Light the candles *after* you set the cake down in front of the birthday child.

Bubbly Ice Cream lemonade. Fill a glass ½ full with
lemonade. Add a scoop of vanilla ice cream and
watch what happens! (It bubbles.)

Decorations

Tape a balloon by its string to each child's seat or to the
edge of the table where each child will sit. Write the
child's name on the balloon with a marker.

Or put balloons on the walls by rubbing them first
against your clothes. If the balloons have names on
them, ask each child to find his or her balloon and
take it to a place at the table.

Anchor a bouquet of balloons to a rock hidden inside a
vase and use it as a centerpiece.

Hang coloured balloons on tree branches for a special
effect outside.

Favours, Prizes, Items for Treat Bags

Balloons, small jars of bubble-blowing liquid, with the wands attached to the inside of the lids, bubble gum, bubble bath.

Inside Games and Activities, Competitive and Noncompetitive

1. Hot Balloon. Play like Hot Potato.
2. Balloon Hunt. Play like a Peanut Hunt. Hunt for deflated balloons. Buy or rent a machine for inflating balloons at the party; blow up everyone's balloons at the hunt.
3. Invite a clown or magician to the party who can make animals by twisting balloons together. Ask that person to make an animal for each child at the party.
4. Musical Balloons
5. Balloon Races, such as the following:

- See how far your inflated balloon goes when you let go of it.
- Who can blow up a balloon the fastest? (This race is for children eight and up.)
- How long can you keep your balloon in the air?
- Who can blow a balloon across the floor first?
- Who can jump to the finish line first with a balloon between the knees?

Outside Activities

1. Make giant bubbles. Mix 8 tablespoons of washing-up liquid with 1 quart of water in a baking tin. Dip a tin can (with both ends neatly and safely removed) into the solution. Slowly pull the can out so that a film of soap remains on one end. Gently blow through the other end. A big bubble should appear. Twist the can to release it into the air. This takes practice. Who will be the first to do it?
2. Give a bottle of commercial bubble mix to each child. Let the children blow bubbles. Good for home movies or video!

TRY AND BLOW THE MOST ENORMOUS BUBBLE EVER SEEN

Cartoon party

Menu

Buy or make a cake that has a cartoon character pictured on it.

Ice cream

Popeye Spinach Milk. Put green food colouring in plain milk.

Optional: Biscuits decorated to look like cartoon characters, such as Snoopy and Mickey Mouse

Decorations

Use old comics and magazines for a tablecloth.

Purchase cups and napkins with cartoon characters on them, or use plain coloured ones.

Let the children draw cartoon characters on the backs of white paper plates or decorate them with cartoon stickers.

Favours, Prizes, Items for Treat Bags

Comic books, markers or crayons, pads of drawing paper, key chains, patches, stickers with cartoon characters on them, flip books

KNOCK, KNOCK. Who's there?
CAR.   CAR WHO?
CARTOON PARTY!

FOR _____

DATE _____

TIME _____

PLACE _____

PHONE _____

P.S: BRING COMICS TO SWAP FOR OTHER COMICS AT MY COMIC SWAP SHOP!

Inside Games and Activities, Noncompetitive

1. Comic-Swap Shop. Have the children bring comics to the party and swap them with each other.
2. Comic-Book Hunt. Roll up comic books, secure them with rubber bands, and hide them, one for each child. Each child can keep the comic book he or she finds. Near the end, ask everyone to hunt for the comics that have not yet been found.

Inside Game, Competitive

Cartoon Relay Race. Each person runs, picks up a pad and crayon, draws a cartoon character, puts the pad and crayon down, and runs back to tag the next person on his or her team. Each player draws on a different page. The first team to finish wins.

Outside Games, Noncompetitive

1. Jerry, Jerry, Tom. Play like Duck, Duck, Goose.
2. Cartoon Man's Buff. Play like Blind Man's Buff but make the sounds of cartoon characters.

Outside Games, Competitive

1. The Blob
2. Run, Rabbits, Run!

Christmas party

Menu

Christmas Tree Cake. Bake cake in a 9-by-13-inch tin. Cool and leave in tin. Frost with pink icing. Let harden. With a toothpick draw a Christmas tree and fill it in with green icing. Decorate the tree with small sweets.

Peppermint-stick ice cream

Juice or milk. If you serve milk in small cartons, the children can use the cartons to make gingerbread houses.

Decorations

Use a Christmas tablecloth, napkins, cups and plates. Giftwrap a box filled with enough chocolates for everyone. Use this as a centrepiece. The children have to guess what's inside the box, and then ask the birthday child to open it and distribute the contents. Give clues to help the children guess.

Hang paper chains over the table.

Favours, Prizes, Items for Treat Bags

Gingerbread biscuits with the children's names on them, jingle bells (tie them on the children's shoes when they come in), Santa Claus stockings, tree decorations, simple homemade aprons with the children's names written on them with a laundry-marking pen, milk-carton gingerbread houses made at the party

Inside Activities, Noncompetitive

1. Make paper chains. On the first link of each chain write the child's name. Attach all the chains together with paper clips and see how far it stretches. At the end of the party, remove the paper clips and give each child his or her part of the chain to take home.

2. Make paper Christmas tree ornaments (older children can try origami designs) and decorate a tree with them.

3. Have Santa Claus visit the party and talk with each child. Take Polaroid pictures to send home with everyone.

4. Make milk-carton gingerbread houses. Each child needs a small, rinsed-out milk carton and a piece of cardboard. Set out assorted coloured sweets, digestive biscuits, and cans of coloured, premixed shop bought icing (homemade icing is not sticky enough). Give the children butter knives and tell them to stick the digestive biscuits onto the milk cartons with the icing to make roofs and sides. Dip the sweets in the icing to decorate the houses.

5. Frost Christmas biscuits and decorate.

Inside Game, Competitive

Guess how many ornaments are on the tree? The child with the closest guess gets a prize.

Outside Game, Noncompetitive

Chocolate Bar Hunt. Play like a Peanut Hunt. Hide one chocolate bar for each child. Everyone keeps the one he or she finds. At the end, ask everyone to help find the missing bars of chocolate.

Outside Game, Competitive

Christmas Scavenger Hunt. Play like a Scavenger Hunt. Listed items to find might be a red bow, a Christmas card with Rudolph on it, a gingerbread biscuit, a piece of wrapping paper with holly on it, a jingle bell, and a bar of chocolate.

Circus party

Menu

Ice Cream Cake (page 148)
Popcorn (for any elephants who come to the party)
Peanuts (for any monkeys who come to the party)
Bananas
Lemonade

Decorations

Give each child two white paper plates, one for food
and one for making a clown face. Provide crayons,
and ask each child to draw a clown face on one of the
paper plates. If possible, put the clown faces in the
middle of the table for everyone to see. Later, make
up each child to look like the clown on his or her
plate.

Tape a balloon to each child's chair or the edge of the
table where he or she will sit. Write the child's name
on the balloon with a marker.

Favours, Prizes, Items for Treat Bags

Clown hats, whistles, bags of crisps, peanuts, popcorn, animal biscuits

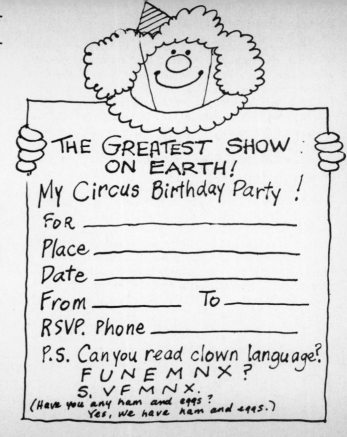

THE GREATEST SHOW ON EARTH!
My Circus Birthday Party!
FOR _____
Place _____
Date _____
From _____ To _____
RSVP. Phone _____
P.S. Can you read clown language?
    F U N E M N X ?
    S. V F M N X.
(Have you any ham and eggs?
Yes, we have ham and eggs.)

Inside Games and Activities, Noncompetitive

1. Have a clown come and help the children put on clown make-up. Be sure it's easy to wash off. The clown can be a friend in disguise.
2. Rehearse a circus show and perform it at the end of the party. Invite parents (ahead of time) to arrive at a certain time to see the show.

Inside Games, Competitive

1. Hot Banana. Play like Hot Potato.
2. Ping-pong Ball Race. Who can push a ping-pong ball across the floor fastest with his or her nose?
3. Peanut Toss. Play like Bull's-Eye Toss.
4. Drop the Peanuts in the Bottle. Play like Drop the Clothespegs in the Bottle.

Outside Games, Noncompetitive

1. Orange Hunt. Play like Peanut Hunt.
2. Animal Biscuit Hunt. Hide one or two animal biscuits for each child. At the end, ask everyone to help find the biscuits that are still hidden.
3. Circus Animal's Buff. Play like Blind Man's Buff but make only circus-animal sounds.

Outside Games, Competitive Circus Stunts

1. Who can stand on one leg the longest?
2. Who can do the most forward somersaults? Backwards?
3. Who can stand on his or her head the longest?
4. Who can toss a ball in the air the longest without dropping it?

CIRCUS SHOW for PARENTS!
1. Rose-tricks on the swing.
2. Beth-juggling balls.
3. Bobby and his dog-tricks.
4. Wayne the clown-jokes.
5. Danny-strongman tricks.
6. Mary, Carol, and Bonnie - a human pyramid.

Barbecue party

Menu

Pigs-in-Blankets (page 154)
Doughboys (page 154)
Celery and carrot sticks
Cupcakes
Toasted marshmallows
Cans of apple juice

Decorations

A picnic table is all that is needed. Make sure there is a
safe place to build a fire and a good way to extin-
guish it afterwards. Make sure there is a safe place
for the children to run around and play. Have
another grownup along to help supervise.

Favours, Prizes, Items for Treat Bags

Frisbies, balls to play with, apples and oranges, bags
of crisps

Note: If it rains, have the picnic inside. Sit on the floor. Put
down a white paper tablecloth and have the children draw ants
crawling over it.

32

Inside Games (in Case of Rain), Noncompetitive

1. Fish for Presents
2. Ring, Ring, Who Has the Ring?
3. Secret Leader
4. Simon Says

Inside Games, Competitive

1. Pin the Tail on the Squirrel. Play like Pin the Tail on the Donkey.
2. Bull's-Eye Toss
3. Camouflage

Outside Games, Noncompetitive

1. Catch (a Frisbie, a ball)
2. Spud
3. Run, Rabbits, Run!
4. The Blob

Outside Games, Competitive

1. Scavenger Hunt
2. Relay Races
3. Dodge Ball or Football
4. Stone

Country fair party

Menu

"Sell" hotdogs, hamburgers, peanuts, popcorn, lemonade, cupcakes, and ice cream cones at a food booth. Have a friend or older child run it. Send food tickets ahead in the post or give them out as the children arrive.

To avoid cooking during the party, just sell peanuts, popcorn, cupcakes, ice cream cones, and lemonade.

Decorations

Using card tables and tents, set up a fairground in your house or outside. Here are some ideas for booths.

- Food Booths
- Fortuneteller's Booth. Ask a friend to dress up as a fortuneteller.
- Game Booths. Ask friends or older children to run them.
- Horror House Booth. Set up a tent. Ask a friend to dress up as a witch who tells children eerie stories and asks them to stick their hands into bowls of "cat's eyeballs" (peeled grapes), "monster brains" (cold spaghetti and oil), "a giant's tongue" (cooked beef tongue), "mice brains" (raisins soaked in water), "toad's eggs" (tapioca). The horror house is best for children ages eight and up.

Favours, Prizes, Items for Treat Bags

Pinwheels, balloons, tickets, play money

Inside Games and Activities, Noncompetitive

1. Fortuneteller.
2. Sock Ball Booth. Children throw sock balls at a grownup's head sticking through a poncho or a sheet of plastic.
3. Polaroid Picture Booth. On a huge piece of cardboard, draw a monster with a wide-open mouth. Cut a head-size hole inside the mouth. A child stands behind the cardboard and sticks his or her head through the hole. A grownup stands in front and snaps a photo of the head in the monster's jaws.

Inside Games, Competitive

1. Raffle. The birthday child draws the name of one of the party guests out of a bag. The winner receives a prize.
2. Penny Pitch Game Booth. Put plates on the floor. Children take turns trying to toss pennies onto them. Each plate counts for different points. Whoever gets the most points wins.

Outside Games and Activities, Noncompetitive

1. Apple Hunt. Play like Peanut Hunt.
2. Spud

Outside Games, Competitive

1. Relay Races
2. Pie-Eating Contest
3. Tug of War
4. Hose the Target. Set up a stepladder on the grass near a garden hose. Put several different-sized stacks of paper cups on a table or sawhorse a distance from the ladder. Ask the children to climb the ladder and try to knock the cups off with water from the hose. Increase the distance and add rocks to the cups to make it harder.

Crazy, upside-down, backwards party

Menu

Crazy Cake. Use the kind of birthday candles that re-light after they are blown out.

Upside-down Ice Cream Cones. Buy flat-bottomed cones. Hold them upside-down and put the scoop of ice cream on top.

Inside-out Sandwiches. Put a slice of bread on the inside and put two slices of meat or cheese on the outside.

Cans of juice or lemonade.

Decorations

Place a paper tablecloth on the floor under the table. Everyone sits *under* the table to eat.

Hang crepe paper streamers *under* the table.

Serve everything backwards. First serve the juice, then the ice cream, then the cake, then, when most of the cake is gone, put candles in the remaining cake and blow them out, singing "You to Birthday Happy."

Favours, Prizes, Items for Treat Bags

Silly Putty, Crazy Straws, markers for making backwards masks at the party

COME TO A **CRAZY** UPSIDE-DOWN BACKWARDS PARTY*

FOR _____

DATE _____

TIME _____

PLACE _____

PHONE _____

P.S. wear your clothes upside down or backwards
And when you come, say good-by.
When you leave, say HELLO!

*written backwards

Inside Games and Activities, Noncompetitive

1. Make backwards masks. Draw the front and back of a head on a paper bag. Cut eyes in the back and wear the paper-bag masks backwards.
2. Have a backwards parade walking in a circle.
3. Write down everyone's name spelled backwards. Try to call each other by his or her backwards name.

Inside Games, Competitive (Winners Lose, Losers Get Prizes!)

1. Backwards Relay Race. Walk or jump backwards.
2. Suitcase Race. Use winter clothes in summer and summer clothes in winter. Put them on backwards.
3. Who can stand on his or her head the longest?
4. Who can do the most backward somersaults?
5. Pin the Nose on the Donkey. Play like Pin the Tail on the Donkey.

Outside Games, Noncompetitive

1. Spud. Call it "Dups" or "Crazy" and spell it that way in the game.
2. Sardines
3. Backward Man's Buff. Play like Blind Man's Buff.

Outside Games, Competitive

1. Backwards Relay Races. Walk or jump backwards.
2. Treasure Hunt. Inside the treasure box there are more clues leading back to the starting point, where the real treasure is.

Dinosaur party

Menu

Dinosaur-Egg Cake. Bake an egg inside the cake. Claim that it is a dinosaur egg. Whoever gets the egg wins a prize.

Dinosaur Ice Cream Cones. Put a small plastic dinosaur on top of each ice cream cone.

Juice, milk, punch

Decorations

Put a plain tablecloth and markers or crayons on the table and have the children draw dinosaurs on it. Ask them to add trees, mountains, sky, and ponds to show what they think the world of dinosaurs looked like.

For a centerpiece, arrange dinosaur toys in a little scene. Add plants and stones to make it realistic. The birthday child may enjoy setting up the arrangement with his or her own toys.

Favours, Prizes, Items for Treat Bags

Various sizes of plastic dinosaurs (small ones are inexpensive by the bagful), markers or crayons to use first on the tablecloth and then to keep.

Inside Activity, Noncompetitive

Make "fossil" handprints for each child to take home. Take several large baking tins of wet sand. Have each child press a hand into the wet sand, then remove it. Pour in quick-drying plaster of paris, made according to the directions on the package. When the handprints are dry, remove them and see if the children can find their own.

Inside Games, Competitive

1. Hot-O-Saurus. Play like Hot Potato but pass around a small dinosaur toy.
2. Pin the Head on the Dinosaur. Play like Pin the Tail on the Donkey.
3. Toss Dinosaurs in the Swamp. Play like Bull's-Eye Toss, only throw plastic or stuffed dinosaurs.

Outside Games, Noncompetitive

1. Dinosaur Hunt. Play like a Peanut Hunt, only hunt for plastic dinosaurs. Have extras to drop near the child who doesn't find any.
2. Duck, Duck, Dinosaur. Play like Duck, Duck, Goose.
3. The Blob

Outside Games, Competitive

1. Red Rover. Say, "Let Susan-O-Saurus come over."
2. Snatch the Dinosaur Egg. Play like Snatch the Flag.
3. Fossil. Play like Stone.

Easter party

Menu

Bunny Rabbit Salad (page 156). Put candles on the one
for the birthday child.
Juice, milk, punch

Decorations

Use flowers as a centrepiece.
At each child's place put a small basket filled with
Easter basket grass and Easter eggs. You can make
the baskets yourself ahead of time. Or for children six
and up, provide tape and construction paper so the
children can make and fill the baskets at the party.

Favours, Prizes, Items for Treat Bags

Easter eggs (decorated at the party), jelly beans, small
chocolate eggs, marshmallow chicks.

Inside Activity, Noncompetitive

Decorate Easter eggs. Cover a table with newspaper. Put out hard-boiled eggs in cartons, crayons, and bowls of dye. To decorate an egg, first draw a design on it with a crayon. Then place the egg on a spoon and dip it into a bowl of dye. The crayon design should show through. Set egg to dry in an upside-down egg carton with the bottoms cut out.

Inside Games, Competitive

1. Hot Egg. Play like Hot Potato but with a plastic or hard-boiled egg.
2. Easter Egg Hunt. Hide all the eggs the children decorated. Wrap one egg with foil. The child who finds that egg gets a prize. As the children find the other eggs, they bring them to a safe place, such as a large Easter basket filled with grass. Afterward, the children can take the eggs they decorated home.

Outside Game, Noncompetitive

Easter Egg Hunt. Hide small chocolate Easter eggs, the kind that are wrapped in brightly coloured foil. Hide enough for everyone to get some. Stand by to drop extras near children who can't find any.

Outside Game, Competitive

Egg Race. See who can walk around the longest holding in his or her mouth a spoon with a hard-boiled or plastic egg on it.

Fairyland party

Menu

Jack-and-the-Beanstalk Cupcakes. Bake a bean in one cupcake. Whoever finds it gets a prize. Tell the child not to eat it.

Ice cream

Juice, milk, punch

Decorations

Put a white paper cloth on the table and give the children crayons or markers so they can draw a fairyland scene. Make up names for the fairyland creatures they draw and write them on the tablecloth.

Favours, Prizes, Items for Treat Bags

Straws and gummed stars. (The children can stick the stars on the tablecloth. They can pretend the straws are magic wands and stick stars on them too.)

COME TO MY
FAIRYLAND BIRTHDAY PARTY
NAME _____
CASTLE _____
DATE _____
FROM _____ TO _____
R.S.V.P.
PHONE _____

Inside Games and Activities, Noncompetitive

1. Make snack necklaces (page 136).
2. Make construction-paper crowns. To make a crown, cut a pointed design along a strip of construction paper. Wrap around the child's head and tape so the crown fits. Make one for each child and put his or her name on it. Decorate with gummed stars.

Inside Game, Competitive

Fairyland Quiz Show. Make a list of questions ahead of time, such as "What are the names of the Seven Dwarfs?" Divide the children into two teams and give prizes to the team that gets the most correct answers. If the children want to continue playing after your questions are used up, ask them to think of more questions.

Outside Games, Noncompetitive

1. The Blob
2. Draw a Circle on the Dragon's Back. Play like Draw a Circle on the Old Man's Back.
3. Ring, Ring, Who's Got the Ring?

Outside Games, Competitive

1. Hunt for Cinderella's Slipper. Hide a fancy shoe. Show the other shoe so the children know what to look for. Whoever finds the missing shoe wins.
2. Giant Steps

Halloween party (can also be a scary party or a monster party)

Menu

Jack-o'-Lantern Cake. Frost a round cake with orange icing and then decorate it with raisins to make a jack-o'-lantern face. The birthday child may like to do this. Each child might also be given a cupcake to frost and decorate to look like a jack-o'-lantern. For a Scary Party or a Monster Party, decorate the cake to look like a monster's face.

Ice cream
Toffee apples
Juice, milk, punch

Decorations

Use a Halloween tablecloth, napkins, cups, and plates. Carve a jack-o'-lantern for the centrepiece. Carve it as soon as the children arrive. Put a candle inside to light when you serve the cake. Turn off the lights when you bring in the cake. Only the jack-o'-lantern and the candles on the birthday cake shine. If you cannot get a pumpkin, use a large turnip.

Favours, Prizes, Items for Treat Bags

Toffee apples. Halloween masks, Halloween sweets, Polaroid pictures of the children in their costumes

Boo-o-o-o! YOU-ooo are invited to my Birthday Halloween Party

Name _____
Place _____
Date _____
Time: from _____ to _____
RSVP. Phone _____

P.S. Bring your costume for a Halloween Parade

Inside Games and Activities, Noncompetitive

1. Ask the children to bring costumes. Have a costume parade. Take pictures.
2. Make paper-bag masks. Provide paper bags, crayons, markers, glue, yarn, and children's scissors. Help the children cut eye holes in the right place.
3. Set up a Horror House. (See Country Fair Party.)
4. Pass the Orange. The children are divided into two teams. The first child in each team puts the orange under his or her chin and passes it to the next child, and so on down the team. The first team to pass the orange all the way down their team is the winner.

Inside Games, Competitive

1. Pin the Hat on the Witch. Play like Pin the Tail on the Donkey.
2. Who Am I? Use names of scary creatures.
3. Hot Potato

Outside Games, Noncompetitive

1. Bob for Apples. (See Apples and Autumn Leaves Party.)
2. Bat, Bat, Dracula. Play like Duck, Duck, Goose.
3. Monster Treasure Hunt. Write the clues on paper cut out in the shape of giant footprints.
4. I Spy

Outside Games, Competitive

1. Giant Steps
2. Run, Rabbits, Run!
3. Snatch the Flag

Kite party

Menu

Kite Cake. Bake cake in a 9-by-13-inch cake tin. Let cool and leave in tin. Frost and let the icing harden. With a toothpick draw a kite and tail on the cake. Fill in the cake with icing of another colour and decorate the tail with gumdrops.

Ice cream

Juice, milk, punch

Decorations

Use a white paper tablecloth. Set out crayons or markers. Ask the children to draw themselves holding a kite floating in the sky. All the kites should be drawn so the tops come together toward the middle of the table. Put each child's name on his or her kite.

Hang real kites from the ceiling.

Favours, Prizes, Items for Treat Bags

Kites: either buy ready-made ones or supply the materials to make kites at the party. See instructions for making paper-bag kites on page 47. Look in the Yellow Pages for names of kite shops.

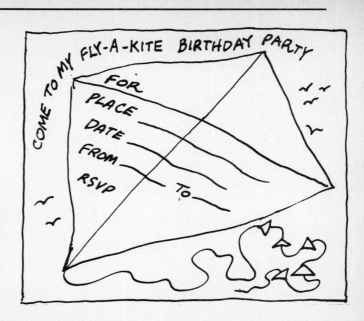

Inside Games and Activities, Noncompetitive

1. Make paper-bag kites for the children to fly later.
2. Make real kites if you can find instructions in a book. (Try the library for good books about kites.) It is complicated to make them, but worth the effort.

Inside Games, Competitive

1. Pin the Kite in the Sky or Pin the Tail on the Kite. Play like Pin the Tail on the Donkey.
2. Hot Kite String. Play like Hot Potato.

Outside Games, Noncompetitive

1. Fly paper-bag kites. Hold the bag behind you and run. Let go of the bag but hold onto the string. Let the string out all the way. The bag should fill up with air and fly.
2. Fly ready-made kites.

Outside Games, Competitive

1. Kite Races. Whoever gets a kite up highest or first wins.
2. Kite Relay Race. The first team to run back and forth holding and passing a kite by its string wins.

MAKE A PAPER BAG KITE:

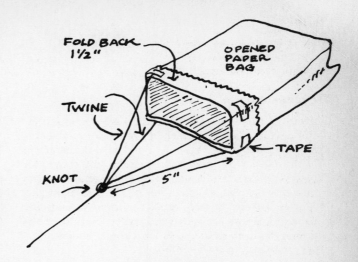

FOLD BACK 1½"

OPENED PAPER BAG

TWINE

TAPE

KNOT

5"

Note: Wide-open space—free from trees and electrical wires—and good winds are needed to fly kites. Drive the children to the park or playground for the party if garden space is lacking, or arrange for everybody to meet at a certain place at an appointed time. The Kite Party can also be given inside without flying kites. Make or give kites for the children to take home.

Make-your-own cupcake party

Menu

Make-Your-Own Cupcakes
Vanilla ice cream
Milk, juice, punch

Decorations

Spread newspaper on the table for easy cleanup later.
Put a paper plate at each child's place. Put one ingredient on each plate. As soon as all the children arrive
at the party, have them go to the table and stand at a
place. Starting with the birthday child, go around the
table, letting each child add his or her ingredient and
stir the batter. Put the cupcakes in the oven and play
games until they are baked and cooled. Have the children come back to the table to frost and eat them.

Favours, Prizes, Items for Treat Bags

Measuring spoons, measuring cups, wooden spoons,
paper chefs' hats, homemade aprons, cupcake
decorations (nuts, raisins, hundreds and thousands, miniature marshmallows)

48

Inside Games, Noncompetitive

1. Sneaky Pete. Put measuring spoons under the
chair.
2. Seven-Up

COME TO MY
MAKE-YOUR-OWN AND
FROST-YOUR-OWN AND
DECORATE-YOUR-OWN
CUPCAKE BIRTHDAY PARTY
NAME
PLACE
DATE
FROM ____ TO ____
good, wait till you think it tastes
come to my party!
Enclosed is a sweet – if you
RSVP. PHONE ____

Inside Games, Competitive

1. Who can make the highest tower of cupcake papers? To do this, put the first one open-side down. Put the next one open-side up. Put the next one open-side down, and so on.

2. Hot Egg. Play like Hot Potato but use a hard-boiled egg.

3. Pin the Candle in the Center of the Cake. Play like Pin the Tail on the Donkey.

Outside Games, Noncompetitive

1. I Spy
2. Kick the Can
3. Red Light, Green Light
4. Cook's Scavenger Hunt. Play like a Scavenger Hunt. Have the children hunt for food and cooking items.

Outside Games, Competitive

1. Red Rover
2. Relay Races. Try to think up some good ones that involve food. For example, ask children to walk while carrying a cup of water on their heads or to walk carrying a hard-boiled egg on a spoon in their mouth. See also Potato Races.

Music and dance party

Menu

Pigs-in-Blankets (page 154)
Watermelon Surprise (page 157)
Make-Your-Own Ice Cream Sundaes and Banana Splits
  (pages 150–151)
Juice, milk, punch

Decorations

Set the table buffet style: plates, forks, spoons, napkins,
Pigs-in-Blankets, mustard, ketchup, and then the
Watermelon Surprise (with the top off—the birthday
child can blow the candles out before you place it on
the table).

Ask the guests to serve themselves. Place a punch bowl
where the children can reach it easily. Later, clear the
table and set out the ingredients for making sundaes
and banana splits.

Favours, Prizes, Items for Treat Bags

Kazoos, toy flutes, toy drums, materials for making musical instruments (an empty coffee can makes a good
drum; a piece of wax paper wrapped around a comb
makes a homemade kazoo—just hold the side of the
comb to the lips and hum)

Music and Dance Activities

1. Invite a good dancer to visit and teach everyone some new dance steps.

2. Invite a musician or band to visit and play.

3. Ask everyone to bring old, unwanted records. Trade them and play them at the party.

Dancing Games and Contests

1. Dance Contest. Give prizes to the best dancers, the fastest dancers, the most creative dancers, the funniest dancers, and so on.

2. Statues. When the music stops, everyone freezes. Whoever moves is out. The last couple or dancer left at the end is the winner.

3. Minute Dance. Ask everyone to stop dancing when he or she thinks a minute is up. Whoever stops closest to sixty seconds after the music started is the winner.

4. Multiplication. One couple starts dancing. When the music stops, they split and pick new partners. When the music starts, the new couples dance. Continue until everyone at the party is dancing.

5. Follow the Leader. Everyone dances the same way as the leader (who is the birthday child at first). Whenever the leader wants, he or she points to a new leader.

Pirate party

Menu

Treasure-Hunt Cupcakes. Write numbered clues on small pieces of paper. Roll them up. Bake one clue in each cupcake. Tell the children to put their clues together to find the treasure, which has been hidden somewhere.
Ice cream
Juice, milk, punch

Decorations

Make a treasure chest for a centrepiece. Cover a cardboard box with foil. Fill it with bags of "gold" (either bags of potato crisps or bags of foil-covered chocolate coins). Connect a string from each bag to each of the children's plates. Then put the cover (also covered with foil) on the box. When the children are seated, remove the cover and have everyone pull his or her string. Afterwards, serve the food.

Favours, Prizes, Items for Treat Bags

Eye patches, headbands, scarves, pirate flags, toy jewellery, snack necklaces (see p. 136), rubber knives, small toy telescopes, chocolate "gold coins"

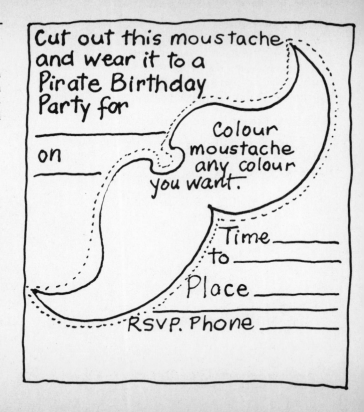

Cut out this moustache and wear it to a Pirate Birthday Party for

_____

on _____

Colour moustache any colour you want.

Time _____
to _____
Place _____
RSVP. Phone _____

Inside Games, Noncompetitive

1. Sneaky Pete
2. Seven-Up
3. Fish for Presents
4. Ring, Ring, Who Has the Ring?

Inside Games, Competitive

1. Camouflage
2. Drop the Clothespegs in the Bottle
3. Treasure Hunt

Outside Games, Noncompetitive

1. Draw a Circle on the Old Man's Back
2. I Spy
3. Kick the Can
4. Sardines

Outside Games, Competitive

1. Red Rover
2. Relay Races. Two pirate teams compete.
3. Snatch the Treasure. Play like Snatch the Flag.

Note: Inside or out, competitive or noncompetitive, a Treasure Hunt should be the main event of this party. The clues might be pieces of a map. The treasure can really be buried. If so, supply shovels to dig it up.

(The clues in their cupcakes will lead them to a hidden eye pencil. When they find it, they'll take turns drawing scars on their faces.)

WARN KIDS AHEAD OF TIME NOT TO EAT CLUES!

53

Powder puff party

Menu

Cake
Ice cream
Juice. Serve in fancy paper cups.

Decorations

Use a fancy paper tablecloth or doilies.
Put paper napkins in napkin rings. Make the rings out
    of cut-up paper-towel rolls.
Use flowers for a centerpiece, either fresh ones or flow-
    ers made from tissue paper and pipe cleaners.
Light candles in candlesticks.

Favours, Prizes, Items for Treat Bags

Children's lipsticks, powders, eye shadows, perfumes,
    mirrors, combs, ribbons, cosmetic bags, costume
    jewellery.

Inside Activities, Noncompetitive

1. After all the children arrive dressed up, give
them make-up to put on. If you like, do not
provide mirrors. Tell them to apply make-up; *then,*

let them look in the mirror. Some will look pretty funny. Later, or whenever you want, help the children remove the make-up with cold cream.

2. Give the children plain paper plates and scraps of ribbons, fabrics, and lace. Tell them to glue these pieces onto the plates to make hats. Tie strings or ribbons to each plate so they can wear them.

3. Have a fashion show. Take pictures or movies.

Inside Games and Activities, Competitive

1. Give prizes for the outfit that is the fanciest, the most original, the funniest, the most colourful, and so on.

2. Pin the Hat on the Lady. Play like Pin the Tail on the Donkey.

Outside Game, Noncompetitive

Cosmetic Hunt. Play like a Peanut Hunt. Hide lipstick, mirror, comb, powder puff, and so on. Hide enough items so every child can find one thing. At the end, ask everyone to look for any missing items.

Outside Game, Competitive

Touch and Feel. Hang socks on a clothesline. Put different items in each one, not necessarily cosmetic things (a paper clip, a sea shell, a screw, a hair-slide). Each child gets a turn to feel and guess what is inside. The child who gets the most right answers wins.

Rainy day party (an emergency plan)

Menu

Whatever was planned for outside can probably be eaten inside. There's usually no need to change your menu.

Decorations

Have the children draw a sunny-day scene on a table covered with a white paper tablecloth, brown paper, white shelf paper, or even old wallpaper, taped to the table back side up.

Cut out a yellow construction-paper sun and hang it on the wall near the tablecloth. Give everyone a sheet of paper and some crayons. Ask everyone to draw one outdoor thing to add to the sun on the wall. As the pictures are finished, display them.

If you were going to go on a picnic, spread a tablecloth on the floor and have everyone pretend he or she is outside, wherever the party was supposed to be. Unload things from the picnic basket. Don't bother to set up a different (nonpicnic) way.

Favours, Prizes, Items for Treat Bags

Give out inside whatever was planned for outside. If the treats are outside treats (balls, squirt guns), be sure to give them out at the end of the party so they aren't used.

IF YOU PLAN AN OUTSIDE PARTY (SUCH AS A BEACH PARTY OR A ROUNDERS GAME), REMEMBER THIS PAGE.

Inside Games, Noncompetitive

1. Sneaky Pete
2. Bull's-Eye Toss (can be competitive)
3. Fish for Presents
4. Treasure Hunt (can be competitive)
5. Ring, Ring, Who Has the Ring?
6. Secret Leader
7. Treat Bag Game
8. Twenty Questions

Inside Games, Competitive

1. Camouflage
2. Drop the Clothespegs in the Bottle (can be non-competitive)
3. Hot Potato (can be noncompetitive)
4. Musical Chairs (can be noncompetitive)
5. Pin the Tail on the Donkey (can be noncompetitive)
6. Simon Says (can be noncompetitive)
7. Statues (can be noncompetitive)
8. Who Am I? (can be noncompetitive)

57

Scientist's party

Menu

Scientist's Cake. Use one of the recipes on page 142 or your own recipe.

Scientist's Ice Cream. Make your own ice cream too.

Scientist's Ice Cream Drink. Fill glasses half full with lemonade. Add a scoop of vanilla ice cream. Watch. What happens? (It bubbles.)

Decorations—Volcano Centerpiece

Make a "volcano" for a centrepiece. Here is how: Take a large roasting tin and fill it with wet sand. Shape most of the sand into a volcano-like mountain, making a hole in the centre that is big enough to hold a large empty frozen-juice can. Make sure the can is not visible. Put 4 tablespoons of baking powder in the can. Cover the table with newspapers. To make the volcano erupt, have the birthday child pour into the hidden can a portion of "magic solution," which is made by mixing 8 fl oz water, 6 fl oz vinegar, 4 fl oz dishwashing liquid, and 10 drops of red food colouring. Watch the volcano erupt and the lava flow. Let the children take turns pouring in a bit of the magic solution to make the volcano erupt.

Favours, Prizes, Items for Treat Bags

Magnets, small magnifiers, printed instructions for making a volcano at home, balloons, seeds, small plants.

SCIENTIST'S BIRTHDAY PARTY

FOR _____

PLACE _____

TIME _____ To _____

RSVP

_____

AT THE PARTY WE WILL MAKE A VOLCANO ERUPT!

Inside Activities, Noncompetitive

1. Make a cake.
2. Make homemade ice cream.
3. Make homemade ice cream drinks.
4. Make a volcano erupt.

Inside Games, Competitive

1. Peanut Hunt. Weigh bags to see who has the most.
2. How Long Is a Minute?
3. Camouflage
4. Hot Potato

Outside Activity, Noncompetitive

Make magic formulas. Give each child a pot or pan and help him collect dirt, twigs, leaves, and flowers to mash and mix with water to make magic formulas. Supervise closely so the children don't pick any poisonous or harmful plants, or eat or drink what they make. Stress that the magic formulas are only make-believe. Write down each child's "recipe" for him or her to take home.

Outside Games, Competitive

1. Scavenger Hunt
2. The Blob
3. Sardines
4. Stone

WET SAND

HIDDEN JUICE CAN

NEWSPAPERS

Stay-the-night party

Menu

Pigs-in-Blankets (page 154)
Bunny Rabbit Salad (page 156)
Cheesecake (page 152)
Punch (page 158)
For breakfast:
   Watermelon Surprise (page 157)
   toast
   fortune pancakes or scrambled eggs
   yogurt
   juice

Decorations

Put a white paper tablecloth on the table and have
  everyone autograph it and draw a self-portrait. Keep
  the tablecloth on the table for breakfast.
In the middle of the table, put things the birthday child
  has made, such as models or clay sculptures.

Favours, Prizes, Items for Treat Bags

Torches, autograph books (the children can make
  them), nightlights, glow-in-the-dark stickers.

60

Inside Games and Activities, Noncompetitive

1. Fortune-teller. Ask a friend to dress as a gypsy and come to the party to tell fortunes. She may ask each child to do something special, such as sing "Jingle Bells," imitate Donald Duck, or stand on his or her head before she will tell the child's fortune.
2. Peanut Hunt
3. Seven-Up

Inside Games, Competitive

1. Treasure Hunt. Hide the treasure in the house.
2. Dancing games. See Music and Dance Party.
3. Who Am I?

Outside Night Games to Be Played in the Semidark

1. Ghost in the Graveyard. Everyone hides. The Ghost (It) goes to find the hidden players. The first person the Ghost comes on yells, "Ghost in the graveyard!" All the players then try to run back to base. The Ghost tries to tag them. The first one tagged is the next Ghost.
2. Torch Tag. Play like regular tag, but to tag someone, shine a torch beam on him or her.
3. Ghost, Ghost. The person who is It counts, "One o'clock, two o'clock . . . twelve o'clock noon! One o'clock, two o'clock . . . twelve o'clock, midnight!" as everyone hides. At "Midnight," It goes to find the hidden players. The first one found and tagged becomes the next It. But It continues to try to find and tag everyone before the next It takes over. Players can run back to base to be safe from It if they want.

Snow party

Menu

Snow Ice Cream. Give each child a large paper cup in which you have placed: 1 teaspoon sugar, 4 fl oz milk, and a scoop of ice cream. Or for a sherbet version, use 4 fl oz orange juice and a scoop of plain yogurt. Ask each child to go out and fill the rest of the cup with clean snow. Bring the cups in, stir the ingredients, and eat!

Hot cocoa with miniature marshmallows

Decorations

Hang paper snowflakes from the ceiling. Make them ahead of time or have the guests help make them at the party. Cut out a large newsprint snowflake for each child's placemat. Print his or her name on it.

Favours, Prizes, Items for Treat Bags

Polystyrene snowballs for an indoor snowball fight, mittens, woolly hats, earmuffs, homemade mufflers.

COME TO A SNOW BIRTHDAY PARTY

FOR ———
PLACE ———
TIME ——— TO ———
RSVP. Phone ———
P.S.: (BRING YOUR mittens, hats boots, coats, sleds, skates, whatever).

Inside Games and Activities, Noncompetitive

1. Make snowflakes and hang them up.
2. Secret Leader
3. Sneaky Pete. Put a polystyrene snowball under the chair.

Inside Games, Competitive

1. Hot Snowball. Play like Hot Potato but use a polystyrene snowball.
2. Bull's-Eye Toss. Use polystyrene snowballs.
3. Mitten Hunt. Hide everyone's mittens during mealtime. The first to find his or her own pair wins. Continue until everyone finds his or her pair.

Outside Games, Noncompetitive

1. Skating, sliding, making snowmen and snow forts.
2. Snowball Tag. Tag someone by hitting him or her with a snowball. Rules: no hitting on the head, no icy snowballs.
3. Make angels in the snow.
4. Colour the snow with food colouring.
5. Build a campfire in an open space and roast potatoes and serve hot chocolate out of a thermos.

Outside Games, Competitive

1. Relay Races
2. Bull's-Eye Toss. Play with snowballs tossed into boxes.
3. Snowman Contest. Give various prizes: best-looking, biggest, smallest, funniest, fattest, and so on.

Space party

Menu

Spaceship Cake. Bake cake in a 9-by-13-inch tin. Frost with blue-tinted icing. Let icing harden. With a toothpick draw, or have your child draw, a spaceship on the icing. Fill in the drawing with white icing and decorate with sweet silver balls and gumdrops.

Vanilla ice cream

Juice, milk, punch. Serve in plastic bags tied with twist ties around straws. Explain that because there is no gravity in space, the juice won't stay down in a cup, and that this is similar to the way astronauts drink beverages.

Decorations

Cover the table with aluminium foil. In the centre place various toy spaceships and spacemen.

Favours, Prizes, Items for Treat Bags

Small toy spaceships, balloons, kites, small plastic spacemen, paper for making paper airplanes, gummed stars

YOU'LL HAVE A BLAST AT A SPACE BIRTHDAY PARTY!

FOR: SPACESHIP COMMANDER

COMMAND BASE (PLACE)

LIFT-OFF TIME _____ To _____

BLAST-OFF DATE

RSVP

IF ALL SYSTEMS GO!

Inside Games and Activities, Noncompetitive

1. Make robots and spaceships out of boxes. Glue on nuts, bolts, smaller boxes, and toilet-paper rolls. If possible, take all the boxes outside and spray them with silver paint while the children are playing. When dry, let the children stick on gummed stars.
2. Space Bag Game. Play like the Treat Bag Game.

Inside Games, Competitive

1. Make paper airplanes and see who can fly one the farthest.
2. Hot Asteroid. Play like Hot Potato.
3. Nuts and Bolts Hunt. Play like a Peanut Hunt. Later on, the children can use their findings for their robots and spaceships. Or let the children trade in what they found for sweets or crisps.

Outside Games, Noncompetitive

1. Spaceman's Buff. Play like Blindman's Buff but make only spaceship sounds.
2. Miss, Miss, Hit. Play like Duck, Duck, Goose.
3. Freeze Tag
4. I Spy

Outside Games, Competitive

1. The Blob
2. Giant Steps
3. Red Rover. Pretend the runners are spaceships.
4. Relay Races. Each team can be a space team.

STRAW

TWIST TIE

JUICE

PLASTIC BAG

IN SPACE, JUICE WOULDN'T STAY IN A CUP. BECAUSE THERE'S NO GRAVITY TO HOLD IT DOWN, IT WOULD FLY ALL OVER THE PLACE. SO, SPACEMEN HAVE TO DRINK OUT OF A SEALED CONTAINER, LIKE THIS ONE.

Tea party for dolls or stuffed animals

Menu

Cake or biscuits
Ice cream
Juice, milk, or weak tea in teacups

For the dolls or stuffed animals:
Play dough for food
Water served in tiny teacups

Decorations

Use one table for the children and a smaller table or
    box for the dolls or stuffed animals. Let your child set
    the small table.
Use two matching sets for tablecloths and napkins.
Use a children's tea set for the big table and a smaller
    toy set for the dolls or stuffed animals.
The children can also hold their toys on their laps and
    "share" with them.

Favours, Prizes, Items for Treat Bags

Toy cups and saucers, bottles for dolls, tiny plastic
    dolls, small stuffed animals, wooden clothespegs
    and scraps of material for making peg-dolls, dolls'
    clothes or old, unwanted baby clothes for dressing
    the dolls.

YOU AND YOUR FAVOURITE
DOLL (OR STUFFED ANIMAL)
ARE INVITED TO MY BIRTHDAY
TEA PARTY

Name ——————
Place ——————
Date ——————
Time: from —— to ——
RSVP.
Phone ——————

Inside Games and Activities, Noncompetitive

1. Sneaky Pete
2. Make dolls' clothes
3. Make clothespeg-dolls
4. Make play dough food. Mix ½ lb flour, 6 oz salt, 1 tablespoon oil, and ¼ pt water. Knead until pliable. Give everyone a ball of dough and ask each child to make pretend food (hot dogs, hamburgers, peas, cake, ice cream cones) for his or her doll or stuffed animal.

Inside Games, Competitive

1. Hot Doll. Play like Hot Potato.
2. Bull's-Eye Toss. Toss stuffed animals.
3. Drop the Clothespegs in the Bottle
4. Musical Chairs

Outside Games, Noncompetitive

1. Toy Man's Buff. Play like Blind Man's Buff but make doll or stuffed animal sounds.
2. Doll Steps. Play like Giant Steps. Make up the steps.
3. Apple Hunt. Play like Peanut Hunt.

Outside Games, Competitive

1. Run, Rabbits, Run!
2. Doll Contest or Stuffed Animal Contest. Give awards for doll or animal that is prettiest, cutest, smartest-looking, most athletic-looking, best dressed, best coiffed, friendliest, and so on. Make sure everyone gets a prize.

Valentine party

Menu

Valentine Cake. Frost a cake with pink frosting. Decorate with small, heart-shaped Valentine sweets.
Peppermint-stick ice cream
Punch made from ginger beer and frozen strawberries
Optional: Heart-shaped biscuits

Decorations

At each place tape a pink balloon with the guest's name written on it with markers. For place mats use large doilies.
Fill paper sweet baskets with Valentine sweets and place one on each doily.
Hang doilies and cut-out hearts from the ceiling.

Favours, Prizes, Items for Treat Bags

Heart-shaped biscuits, heart-shaped biscuit cutters, sweet baskets, materials for making Valentines.

Valentine's Birthday Party

For _____
Place _____
Time _____ to _____
Date _____
R S V P
Phone

2 Good 2B   4 Gotten

Inside Game and Activity, Noncompetitive

Valentine Treat Box Game. Decorate a big cardboard box to look like a Valentine box. Cut arm holes in each side. Fill the box with small treats (potato crisps, chocolate, lollipops, toy cars, toy airplanes, comic books). To play, a blindfolded guest reaches in the box, feels something, pulls it out, holds it up, and must identify it in order to keep it.

Inside Games, Competitive

1. Hot Valentine. Play like Hot Potato but pass around a Valentine card.
2. Valentine Contest. Give a prize for the Valentine that is prettiest, funniest, best rhymed, and so on. Make sure everyone gets a prize.

Outside Games, Noncompetitive

1. Valentine Hunt. Play like a Peanut Hunt. Hide a Valentine for everyone. The names should be clearly marked on the outside of the envelopes. Guests find their own cards and leave the others untouched. At the end everyone hunts for the cards still missing.
2. Sardines

Outside Game, Competitive

Valentine Scavenger Hunt. Play like a Scavenger Hunt. Collect things for making Valentines: lace, yarn, doilies, hearts, gold stars, tape, glue, silver and gold paper, and so on.

Zoo party

Menu

Animal Cake. Bake and frost a cake. Decorate it with
biscuits frosted in contrasting colours.
Ice cream cones
Juice, milk, punch

Decorations

Cover the table with newspaper. With a black marker
draw big stripes across the table. As the guests come
in ask them to draw zoo animals behind the black
bars. Provide crayons and coloured markers.
Put a box of animal biscuits at each place, with the
child's name on it.

Favours, Prizes, Items for Treat Bags

Animal biscuits, chocolates, rubber snakes, small
plastic zoo animals, crayons, markers, pipe cleaners

Inside Games and Activities, Noncompetitive

1. Make animal masks from paper bags. Provide construction paper, children's scissors, crayons, tape, pipe cleaners, paste.

2. Make animals from pipe cleaners and then make paper cages for them. Set up a little table-top zoo.

Inside Games, Competitive

1. Peanut Hunt
2. Pin the Trunk on the Elephant. Play like Pin the Tail on the Donkey.
3. Drop the Peanuts in the Elephant's Trunk. Play like Drop the Colthespegs in the Bottle.

Outside Game, Noncompetitive

Animal Biscuit Hunt. Play like a Peanut Hunt. Hide as many boxes of biscuits as there are children at the party. At the end everyone hunts for the hardest-to-find boxes so that everyone has one to keep.

Outside Games, Competitive

1. May I? Play like Giant Steps. Make up various animal steps for the game.
2. Red Rover. Pretend to be animals trying to get out of cages.
3. Relay Races. Have animal names for each team.

Chapter 3

Games

The key factor to successful birthday parties for children is the selection of age-appropriate games. If you pick games that are too challenging, the children become frustrated and unhappy. If you pick games that are too easy, the children become bored.

If you don't have much time to spend on party preparations, skip the crepe paper and concentrate on selecting several games that are right for the children coming to the party. If the children are between the ages of four and six, select noncompetitive games or devise noncompetitive ways to play standard competitive games, such as Pin the Tail on the Donkey and Drop the Clothespegs in the Bottle. For this age group, play games so that everybody wins. Either skip prizes altogether, or give one to everyone.

For children seven to ten, competitive games are fun, but keep in mind that seven-year-olds are just beginning to gain the maturity needed to suffer defeat. Go easy on them. Remember that birthday parties are supposed to be enjoyable for everyone. Eight-year-olds, nine-year-olds, and ten-year-olds understand contests, will follow rules, have team spirit, and give their all to win. Save your competitive games for them. Children in this age group also love noncompetitive games like Sardines and Draw a Circle on the Old Man's Back, in which there is much hiding and chasing.

If you're planning an outdoor party, have a list of inside games you can play when the drops begin to fall. (See Rainy Day Party on page 56.)

As you select games, remember that many of the inside games can be played outside and some of the outside games can be played inside, and that there are ways to turn a competitive game into a noncompetitive one. Many such noncompetitive versions are listed.

Go over the games with your child. Agree ahead of time on the ones you both think would be fun. If you are not sure they will work, ask your child's teacher. I have found that teachers give good advice about age-appropriate games, and I'm grateful for the kindergarten teacher who once told me when I asked her about games for five-year-olds, "Don't play any competitive ones." At first I thought she was being "too nice," but I took her advice anyway, and the resulting party was probably one of the best ones we ever had.

Old favourites, such as Musical Chairs, are part of the tradition of birthday parties. Often you can give them a new name to fit the theme of the party (Dinosaur Chairs, Mad Scientists' Chairs). As you help children play games, keep in mind that not all children may want to play. They may prefer to play with toys or just to watch. Don't make them play. At a large party as many as half of the children may prefer "free time" over organized games. As long as they're supervised, this is fine.

The age levels recommended for these games are only that—recommendations. You know your child best, so use your own judgment. In general, it's better to play games that are too easy than games that are too hard.

Games and Activities for Toddlers. Keep games short and simple for very young children. (1) Try singing games, such as Mulberry Bush, Ring-a-Ring-a-Roses, and I'm a Little Teapot. If your children are in a playgroup, find out what games they play there and learn how to play them. Learn the songs or have the children at the party teach them to you. (2) Sit in a circle and do finger-play games, such as Itsy Bitsy Spider, This Little Piggy, and Pat-a-Cake, Pat-a-Cake. (3) Have the children sit in a circle with their legs spread out and toes touching and roll a beach ball back and forth. Call out the name of each child who touches it. (4) Have a parade in your house. Give each child spoons to bang together or coffee-can drums to pat. March all around the house. (5) Turn the parade into Follow the Leader. Let different children be the leader, starting with the birthday child. (6) Have everyone lie down on the floor and get comfortable. See who can be quiet the longest.

Games for Children 4–6. The hardest lesson I have learned is not to have competitive games for children four to six years old. *They can't take losing.* Even seven-year-olds find it rough, but at least they can swallow their disappointment and cope. Younger children can't. Their outlook on the world is basically egocentric. When you say "contest," each one of them thinks he or she will win and is crushed by defeat. It's unfair to expect more of children this age. Their egocentricity is a phase they will outgrow. There is no need to toughen them up before their time; there is especially no need to test children's toughness at birthday parties.

The trick with four-to-six-year-olds is to take favourite games, such as Pin the Tail on the Donkey, and play them in a noncompetitive way. Look at the game from a five-year-old's point of view. It's fun to be blindfolded, turned about, and told to tape your tail to a donkey on the refrigerator. It's fun when your turn is over to have someone comment on the special place you have put the tail: "Johnny put his tail on the donkey's ear!" It's fun to watch where the other tails land. Okay, so someone tapes the tail in the right place. An adult can then say, "Look where Kenny put his tail! Exactly where real donkey tails go!" Everyone will be pleased. There is no need to ruin the mood by giving Kenny, and Kenny only, a prize. Give everyone a prize or no one. Or just avoid games that beg for a winner. Children *at this age* will be happier with this arrangement.

Children in the four-to-six age group like to play games like tag, where everyone gets a chance to be It and there is no one overall winner. Other good, noncompetitive games for this age group are Duck, Duck, Goose, Drop the Handkerchief, a Peanut Hunt (in which every child keeps the peanuts he or she finds and you have a pocketful ready to drop near the child who can't find any), and Giant Steps (good for this age group because you can rig the game so everyone wins once).

Play Musical Chairs, but when someone is left without a chair, just say, "This time Marie is left standing!" Do not remove a chair. Marie goes back in the game. Next time someone else will be left standing. The fun, in other words, is seeing who's left standing each time, not in eliminating players to find a winner.

Games for Children 7-10. Children seven and older can play organized games well. They can win and lose (tens can do this better than sevens, though). They like to play real games with teams, like rounders, and football, where you referee. Children this age love to run relays and go on treasure hunts and scavenger hunts. I have found that the easiest way to plan a party for them is to ask the birthday child to plan the games ahead of time, choosing from the games he or she already knows from school. This is fun for the child, nice for me and you. No headaches.

It's also helpful to ask your child's classroom or gym teacher for game suggestions. Once you've got a list of good games, you can relax about the party. Chances are, it will go well.

To end a party successfully, try to organize games so that the children are psychologically ready to leave. The last game might be Find the Jackets, which you have hidden, or a Treasure Hunt for the treat bags. Treat bags are often given out as children are leaving, so that they have something of their own to take with them.

Blind Man's Buff

Age Level: 5 and up
Number of Players: 3 or more
What Is Needed: a blindfold
Type of Game: noncompetitive
Location: inside or outside

How to Play

Blindfold It (the birthday child at first). Spin It around several times, then stop. The other players move around It, making funny sounds as It tries to tag them. The first person tagged becomes It.

Variations

Change the name of the game and specify the sounds to be made. For example, in Astronaut's Buff, tell the players to make only spaceship sounds.

The Blob

Age Level: 4 and up
Number of Players: 6 or more
What Is Needed: nothing
Type of Game: competitive or noncompetitive
Location: outside

How to Play

The birthday child is the Blob. The Blob chases the players. Whoever the Blob catches has to hold the Blob's hand and run with him or her to catch other players. In other words, players who are tagged become part of the Blob. When the Blob contains as many as four players, it can split in half to form two Blobs. Both Blobs can now catch players.

Competitive Version

The last child to be caught is the winner.

Noncompetitive Version

The last child to be caught becomes the next Blob.

THE BLOB →

Bull's-Eye Toss

Age Level: 3 and up

Number of Players: 3 or more

What Is Needed: things to toss (beanbags, stuffed animals, balls, peanuts in their shells), and baskets or cartons to catch them

Type of Game: competitive or noncompetitive

Location: inside or outside

How to Play

Have the children stand behind a line on the floor or ground. Set the basket (or baskets, each one worth a different amount of points) far enough away to be challenging to the children but not impossible to hit. For younger children, it helps to have several baskets, one quite close, so that most of them can experience shooting a bull's-eye.

Competitive Version

The children who get the most points compete in a playoff with the baskets farther away.

Noncompetitive Version

Let the children take turns throwing the objects until they tire of the game. Count up points for each child. See whether the child can beat his or her score on subsequent turns.

Variations

Change the name to suit the theme of the party: Toss the Dinosaur in the Swamp for a Dinosaur Party, and so on.

Camouflage

Age Level: 7 and up

Number of Players: 4 or more

What Is Needed: items to hide (a ring, stamp, thimble, hairpin, paper clip, pencil, button, coin, rubberband, matchstick); for each player, a list of the hidden items and a pencil

Type of Game: competitive

Location: inside

How to Play

Before the party, hide all the items in plain sight but against camouflaged backgrounds in one room. For example, place a copper penny on a copper lamp, a green stamp on a green book, a multicoloured stamp on a floral curtain, and a yellow pencil on a yellow couch. Tell the children, "You may not touch anything. Everything is in plain sight, but you have to look very, very carefully to see it. When you see something on your list, check it off. But first walk away so other players don't see where you found it. Keep your list to yourself. The first person who finds all the items wins. But everyone will have a chance to finish." There should be a first prize, a second prize, a third prize, and a booby prize. At the end of the game, the first players to finish help the last ones by giving them verbal clues.

Detective

Age Level: 6 and up
Number of Players: 4 or more
What Is Needed: nothing
Type of Game: noncompetitive
Location: outside

How to Play

Establish a home base. It (the birthday child at first) is the Detective. The Detective counts to 60 out loud, as the other players hide. Then the Detective goes to find them. When the Detective comes on someone, that player tries to run back to base without being tagged. If the Detective tags the player, that player becomes a Detective. Eventually almost everyone is a Detective. The last one to be caught is the first Detective in the next game.

Dodge Ball

Age Level: 4 and up
Number of Players: 16–30
What Is Needed: a large ball for throwing (a beach ball or football)
Type of Game: competitive or noncompetitive
Location: outside

How to Play

Divide the children into two teams. One team makes a circle and the other team stands inside it. The players forming the circle throw the ball at the players inside the circle, who are running around trying not to get hit. The inside players may not catch the ball. A ball hitting a player on the head does not count. Only players in the outside circle may throw and catch the ball. Players who get hit join the outside circle and help them try to hit the players remaining inside.

Competitive Version

The last player left inside the circle is the winner.

Noncompetitive Version

Each player who gets hit trades places with the person who hit him or her. The game continues until the children tire of it.

Draw a Circle on the Old Man's Back

Age Level: 6 and up
Number of Players: 4 or more
What Is Needed: nothing
Type of Game: noncompetitive
Location: outside

How to Play

It (the Old Man) covers his or her eyes and leans up against a tree or wall. A second child chants, while drawing a circle with a finger on Its back, "Draw a circle on the old man's back, and somebody lightly taps," then points in silence to another child. This third child steps forward and taps It on the back. It tries to guess who tapped. If It guesses correctly, the tapper becomes It. If It guesses incorrectly, everyone says, "No." Then It counts out loud to 100, eyes still closed, and the other players scatter and hide. It goes to find the other players. If It finds a player, the player must stay with It and go with It to find others. The last person found becomes the next It (Old Man).

" DRAW A CIRCLE ON THE OLD MAN'S BACK, AND SOMEBODY LIGHTLY TAPS."

Drop the Clothespegs in the Bottle

Age Level: 4 and up

Number of Players: 2 or more

What Is Needed: bottle or jar (a wide-mouth jar is good for younger children), clothespegs or other things to drop (peanuts in their shells, Tinkertoys, buttons)

Type of Game: competitive or noncompetitive

Location: inside

How to Play

The children take turns seeing how many clothespegs they can drop in the bottle. The rules are to hold the clothespeg with a straight arm at shoulder height or with a bent arm at waist height (just make sure everyone does it the same way) and to stand straight (no one can bend over).

Competitive Version

The child who drops the most clothespegs in the bottle wins.

Noncompetitive Version

Let the children take turns dropping clothespegs into the bottle until they tire of the game. Each child does his or her best each time and tries to beat his or her own record.

Duck, Duck, Goose

Age Level: 4 and up
Number of Players: 5 or more
What Is Needed: nothing
Type of Game: noncompetitive
Location: inside or outside

How to Play

The children sit in a circle. It (the birthday child at first) walks around the outside of the circle tapping each child on the head lightly, saying "Duck" with each tap until It finally taps a player and says "Goose!" The Goose then jumps up and chases It around the outside of the circle, trying to tag him or her before It reaches the empty space. If It gets there first, the Goose becomes the next It. If Goose catches It, the same child is It again.

Variations

This is a very good game for children four to six. Change the name to suit the party's theme: Bat, Bat, Dracula for a Halloween Party or Miss, Miss, Hit for a Space Party or Rounders Party, and so on.

Everyone's It

Age Level: 4 and up
Number of Players: 5 or more
What You Need: nothing
Type of Game: noncompetitive
Location: outside

How to Play

When the parent says, "Go!" every child is It and runs around tagging anyone he or she can catch. If you are tagged you must stop, stand still, and put your hands on your head. Soon there will be only a few players left. Everyone watches them stalk and chase each other until only one is left. He or she gets to say, "Go!" for the next round. This is a great game for a large group of kids!

Fish for Presents

Age Level: 3 and up
Number of Players: 2 or more
What Is Needed: a "fishing pole" (a branch or stick with a string tied to it and a cup hook or hook bent from a paper clip tied to the end of the string); a large box or small plastic swimming pool for a "pond"; presents wrapped in paper and ribbon
Type of Game: noncompetitive
Location: inside or outside

How to Play

Each child has a turn to fish for a present, which is snared when the hook catches onto a bow. (Make sure the bows are "catchable.") The child lifts the present out of the pool with the fishing pole and keeps the present.

It's a good idea for the presents to be things the children can use at the party: crayons, Matchbox cars, water pistols, jars of bubble-blowing liquid, and so on.

Freeze Tag

Age Level: 4 and up
Number of Players: 4 or more
What Is Needed: nothing
Type of Game: noncompetitive
Location: outside

How to Play

It (the birthday child at first) runs around trying to tag other players. Anyone who is tagged must "freeze" (hold still). However, any other player may "melt" a frozen player by touching him or her. A "melted" player can resume running around again to avoid It. Whoever is tagged ("frozen") three times is the next It.

Game for opening presents

Age Level: 4 and up
Number of Players: 3 or more
What Is Needed: presents
Type of Game: noncompetitive
Location: inside or outside

How to Play

As guests arrive, ask them to put their presents in a pile. When everyone has come, have everyone sit around the pile of presents. The birthday child stands in the middle, selects a present, and reads the card (or has it read). Then the birthday child and the others try to guess what is inside the present. The gift giver may give up to three clues to help them guess. After the clues are used up or after someone guesses correctly, the birthday child opens the present.

Giant Steps (also called: May I?)

Age Level: 4 and up
Number of Players: 3 or more
What Is Needed: nothing
Type of Game: competitive (sort of)
Location: outside

How to Play

Establish a start and finish line. The leader (usually an adult for young children, but this could be the birthday child) stands behind the finish line. The children spread out across the start line. The leader gives the first command, such as "David, you may take three baby steps." David then *must* ask, "May I?" If he doesn't say this, his turn is over. If he does, the leader can say, "Yes, you may," in which case David then takes three baby steps toward the finish line. The leader can arbitrarily change his or her mind and give another command: "No, you may not. You may take five giant steps." Again, David *must* ask, "May I?" If the leader says, "Yes, you may," David moves five giant steps toward the finish line. The first child to reach the finish line wins, but since the leader can manipulate the game so that certain children win, this is a good game to soothe unhappy children. Various steps are baby steps, giant steps, hops, jumps, twirl steps, backwards steps, and leaps. Make up new ones.

93

Hot Potato

Age Level: 3 and up
Number of Players: 4 or more
What Is Needed: a potato, a radio or record or tape player for music
Type of Game: competitive or noncompetitive
Location: inside or outside

How to Play

Have the children sit in a circle close together. Give the birthday child a potato and ask him or her to start passing it when you start the music. When you stop the music, whoever has the potato holds it up.

Competitive Version

Whoever is left holding the potato when the music stops is out and must leave the circle. Everyone closes in, and the game resumes. Eventually there are only two children left. The next time the music stops, the one who is not holding the potato wins. Rule: No one is allowed to throw the potato when the music stops. Anyone who does is automatically out.

Noncompetitive Version

When the music stops, whoever has the potato is out. You say, "Mary has it!" and everyone laughs. Mary does not have to leave the circle. Play until the children tire of the game.

Variations

Change the name to suit the theme of the party: Hot Egg for an Easter Party or Hot Balloon for a Balloon Party, and so on.

How Long Is a Minute?

Age Level: 3 and up

Number of Players: 2 or more

What Is Needed: a stopwatch or clock or watch with a second hand

Type of Game: competitive or noncompetitive

Location: inside or outside

How to Play

Ask the children to sit down and shut their eyes. Tell them that when you say, "Go," they should start counting slowly to 60 because there are 60 seconds in a minute. As soon as they think one minute is up, they are to raise their hands.

Competitive Version

Whoever raises his or her hand 60 seconds later, or closest to 60 seconds later, wins.

Noncompetitive Version

Whoever raises his or her hand 60 seconds later, or closest to 60 seconds later, is congratulated. Then players shut their eyes and try again. Play until the children tire of the game.

THIS IS A GOOD GAME TO HELP CHILDREN RELAX AND SETTLE DOWN. IT IS A BLESSEDLY QUIET GAME.

I Spy

Age Level: 8 and up
Number of Players: 5 or more
What Is Needed: nothing
Type of Game: noncompetitive
Location: outside

How to Play

It (the birthday child at first) closes his or her eyes in a certain spot called "Jail" and counts to 50 or 100 as the other players hide. Then, It goes to seek them. When It sees someone, It runs back to Jail and yells, "I spy Danny under the lilac bush," or whatever. Danny then has to come out and stay in Jail. It goes off to search for other players. While It is searching, other players can run to Jail and free anyone there by touching him or her and yelling, "I free Danny!" If It tags this would-be liberator in the act of trying to free others, the caught person must go to Jail. The last player to be caught becomes the next It.

Kick the Can

Age Level: 7 and up
Number of Players: 4 or more
What Is Needed: a tin can
Type of Game: noncompetitive
Location: outside

How to Play

Establish a small area called "Jail" (often it is the middle of the lawn). Place a tin can in the Jail. It (the birthday child at first) gets a running start and kicks the can as far as he or she can. As soon as the can is kicked, the other players run and hide. It retrieves the can, brings it back to Jail, and counts to 50 or 100. Then It sets out to find the hidden players. When It spots one, It runs back to the can and yells, "I see Ned behind the tree!" Ned must surrender and come to Jail. When the last player is captured, another round is begun with the first player captured as the new It.

At any point while It is out hunting, a player can run to Jail and free all the prisoners there with the cry, "All-ee-all-ee-in-free!" The rescuer then kicks the can as far as he or she can, and It must come back, retrieve it, and start counting all over again. This game can go on a long time!

97

Musical Chairs

Age Level: 4 and up
Number of Players: 5 or more
What is needed: a radio or record or tape player for music, as many chairs (the sturdier the better) as there are players, minus one
Type of Game: competitive or noncompetitive
Location: inside

How to Play

Put the chairs in a row in the middle of a cleared-out space. Face every other chair the opposite way, or put two rows of chairs back to back. Have the children stand in a circle around the chairs. When the music starts, the children walk (not run) around the chairs. When the music stops, they sit down. One child will be left standing. Do not let the game get wild.

WARNING:
Children have got hurt in this game, falling on their backsides when chairs were slipped out from under them, so it's important to supervise this game and see that the children don't get carried away.

Competitive Version

The child who is out leaves the circle, and a chair is removed. Children who are out of the circle can dance to the music, if they like. Continue playing until there are two players left and only one chair. Whoever sits on it when the music stops is the winner.

Noncompetitive Version

Don't remove chairs. Whoever is left standing each time gets a good laugh: "This time it's Matthew!" That's all. Matthew doesn't have to leave the game.

Variation: Musical Balloons

Children bat around balloons (as many as there are children minus one). When the music stops, see who's left without a balloon. Rule: you can't catch a balloon until the music stops. If you play competitively, let the child who's out pop a balloon so there will be one less.

Peanut Hunt

Age Level: 4 and up
Number of Players: 2 or more
What Is Needed: peanuts (or other things) to hide, paper bags
Type of Game: competitive or noncompetitive
Location: inside or outside

How to Play

Before the guests arrive, or while they are eating or being otherwise entertained, hide peanuts in one room or outside on the lawn. Before the hunt begins, define the borders of the area where the peanuts are hidden. Give each child a bag to hold the peanuts he or she finds. The birthday child can give the signal for the hunt to begin. Change the name of the hunt by hiding other objects: Valentines, Easter eggs, chocolates, nuts and bolts, and buttons. Often the found objects can lead to another activity, such as gluing nuts and bolts onto cardboard boxes to make spaceships and robots, or making button jewellery.

Competitive Hunt

The children count what they've found. Whoever has the most wins.

Noncompetitive Hunt

The players keep what they've found. Extra peanuts are dropped near any child who has trouble finding them.

Pin the Tail on the Donkey

Age Level: 4 and up
Number of Players: 2 or more
What Is Needed: a picture of a donkey (you can make it or buy it) taped to the refrigerator or a door, a tail, tape or pins, a blindfold
Type of Game: competitive or noncompetitive
Location: inside

How to Play

Put a piece of tape or a pin on the end of the tail. Blindfold the birthday child (who goes first) and spin him or her around three or four times. Then head the child in the right direction and ask the child to stick the tail on the donkey. Wherever the child sticks the tail, write the child's name. Remove the tail for the next child's turn. Continue until everyone has had a turn.

Competitive Version

The child who puts the tail in the most correct spot wins.

Noncompetitive Version

Talk about each place the tail got put: "Johnny put his on the eye!" Laugh together at such silliness, and at the end say congratulations to the child who put the tail in the most realistic spot. Don't make a big fuss about it.

Variations

Change the name of the game to suit the theme of the party: Pin the Hat on the Witch for a Halloween Party or Pin the Head (or Tail) on the Dinosaur for a Dinosaur Party, and so on.

Potato Races

Age Level: 7 and up
Number of Players: 2 or more
What Is Needed: 1 potato and 1 spoon for each player
Type of Game: competitive
Location: outside or inside

Race 1: Potato Jump Race

Establish a start and finish line. Line the children up on the start line. Give the children potatoes to put between their thighs. Say, "Ready, on your mark, get set, *go*," and see who can jump to the finish line first without dropping the potato.

Race 2: Potato Spoon Race

Establish a start and finish line. Line the children up on the start line. Give the children potatoes and spoons and show them how to hold the spoon in their mouths and carry the potato on it. Say, "Ready, on your mark, get set, *go*," and see who can get to the finish line first without dropping the potato or the spoon.

These games may require different-sized potatoes: large ones for the Potato Jump Race and smaller ones for the Potato Spoon Race. Tennis balls and Ping-Pong balls can also be used. These two races combine well with the game Hot Potato.

Red Light, Green Light

Age Level: 4 and up
Number of Players: 3 or more
What Is Needed: nothing
Type of Game: noncompetitive
Location: outside

How to Play

Establish a start and finish line. It (the birthday child at first) stands at the finish line. The other players spread out across the start line. It yells, "Green Light!" turns away from the players, and counts out loud from one to ten, during which time the players run toward the finish line. When It reaches ten, It yells, "Red Light!" and turns back to the players. At the sound of the words "Red Light," the players stop running and freeze. It (or an adult standing on the sidelines) sends anyone still moving back to the start line. It yells, "Green Light!" and the game continues. Eventually someone reaches the finish line and touches It. That person is the next It.

Red Rover

Age Level: 6 and up
Number of Players: 6 or more
What Is Needed: nothing
Type of Game: competitive (sort of)
Location: outside

How to Play

Divide the players into two teams. The teams link arms and stand opposite each other about fifty feet apart. The birthday child should be at the end of one line so he or she can go first, naming a child (let's say Janie) on the other team this way: "Red Rover, Red Rover, let Janie come over." Janie then runs across the play area and tries to break through the chain of opposite players. If she breaks through, she goes back to her own team. If she doesn't, she joins the team she couldn't break through. Theoretically, the last person to join a chain is the winner, but often the game doesn't get this far. Play just until the children feel like playing something else.

Relay Races

Age Level: 7 and up
Number of Players: 6 or more
What Is Needed: props for some of the races
Type of Game: competitive
Location: outside

How to Play

Divide the children into teams by numbering off: with two teams, count off by twos; with three teams, count off by threes, and so on. If a team is short a player, have one of the players run twice. This could be the birthday child. Establish clear start and finish lines. Have the teams line up behind the start lines. Say, "Go!" The first member of each team runs from start line to finish line and back, doing whatever is required. He or she taps the next player, who then does the same thing. The first team to have all its players back wins.

The success of relay games depends on the age of the children. They must be old enough to obey rules and accept defeat. Success also depends on the firmness of the adult running the games. Keep strict rules: no pushing ahead of the start line, no skipping requirements. If the teams seem unfairly balanced, switch players until the teams are comparable. Announce which team wins each competition, and keep a tally to establish which team wins the most points. The members of the best team overall can get blue ribbons tied around their upper arms or pieces of blue tape on their shirts.

Various Races

1. Bell Race. Use a cowbell (or other noisemaker) for each team, placed on the finish line. Requirement: run to the finish line, ring the bell, put it down, run back.

2. Crawling Race. No props needed. Requirement: crawl on all fours to the finish line and back.

3. Draw-a-Face Race. Put a crayon and a pad of paper on the finish line for each team. Requirement: each child runs to the finish line, draws his or her face on the pad, signs his or her name, turns the page, puts the pad and crayon back down on the finish line, runs back.

4. Running Backwards Race. No props needed. Requirement: run backwards to the finish line and back.

5. Somersault Race. No props needed. Requirement: somersault in as straight a line as possible to the finish line and run back.

6. Suitcase Race. Fill a suitcase (or shopping bag) with funny clothes for each team. Requirement: run with the suitcase to the finish line, open it, put on the clothes, bow (teammates must bow back), take off the clothes, put them back, close the suitcase, and run back with it.

7. Three-Legged Race. The members of each team pair off. Tie the inside legs of each pair with heavy string or cloth ties. Requirement: each three-legged pair runs/walks to the finish line and back. If you fall, get up and continue.

8. Wheelbarrow Race. No props needed. Requirement: one child holds the feet of another, who walks on his or her hands to the finish line and back.

Ring, Ring, Who Has the Ring?

Age Level: 5 and up
Number of Players: 6 or more
What Is Needed: a ring, a button, or a washer strung on
a string that is long enough to go around the circle
the children form
Type of Game: noncompetitive
Location: inside or outside

How to Play

Have all the children form a circle around It (the birthday child first). Give them the circle of string and have
them stand back with their arms out and touching,
holding the string taut. The ring should be hidden in
one player's hand. (Ask It to close his or her eyes while
the ring is hidden.) The children keep sliding their
hands back and forth along the string, secretly passing
the ring along. Once they have the knack of this, It can
open his or her eyes and try to guess who has the ring.
If It guesses correctly, the person who has the ring becomes the next It. If It guesses incorrectly, the game
continues.

Run, Rabbits, Run!

Age Level: 5 and up
Number of Players: 5 or more
What Is Needed: nothing
Type of Game: competitive or noncompetitive
Location: outside

How to Play

The birthday child picks one or two other children to be "foxes." They go and sit in a "foxhole" at the far end of the playing area, with their backs toward everyone. The rest of the children are "rabbits." They line up at the other end of the playing area, facing the backs of the foxes. When a grownup says, "Rabbits, go and eat," the rabbits creep across the playing area toward the foxes. When the grownup yells, "Run, rabbits, run!" the foxes jump up and chase the rabbits back to their starting line. Any rabbits who are caught by foxes become foxes.

Competitive Version

Play until there is only one rabbit left—the winner.

Noncompetitive Version

The last rabbit left takes the grownup's place, giving the commands "Rabbits, go eat" and "Run, rabbits, run!" Play until the children tire of the game.

Scavenger Hunt

Age Level: 8 and up
Number of Players: 6 or more
What Is Needed: for each team a list of things to find and a shopping bag
Type of Game: competitive
Location: outside

How to Play

Divide the children into teams of three to four children each. Give each team a list (all the lists are the same), and tell the teams where they can go to find the objects. Each team gets a separate territory. Give the children a time limit (such as a half an hour), and be sure one member of each team has a watch or will be in charge of asking the time. The team that finds the most items on the list *in the allotted time* wins.

When making up the lists, include things the children stand a good chance of finding. For a neighborhood, some suggestions are a stamp, a four-hole button, a biscuit, a straw, a rubber band, a penny dated in the sixties, a hairpin, and last Sunday's newspapers. For a rural area or a park, some suggestions are a pine cone, a worm, a bug, moss, a white rock, something red, a piece of litter, a feather.

Variations

Change the name of the game to suit the theme of the party: Leaf Scavenger Hunt for an Apples and Autumn Leaves Party, Beach Scavenger Hunt for a Beach Party, and so on.

Secret Leader

Age Level: 5 and up
Number of Players: 4 or more
What Is Needed: nothing
Type of Game: noncompetitive
Location: inside

How to Play

It (the birthday child at first) leaves the room. Then everyone sits in a circle and an adult appoints a secret leader. The secret leader starts a motion, such as clapping hands or snapping fingers, and everyone copies. It is called back into the room and tries to guess who the secret leader is. The secret leader keeps changing motions. These are always copied by everyone else. The leader is hard to spot because the other children in the circle try to fool It by looking at the secret leader as little as possible or by looking at someone else. When It guesses the leader correctly, the leader becomes It, and a new secret leader is appointed.

Seven-Up

Age Level: 4 and up
Number of Players: 5 or more
What Is Needed: nothing
Type of Game: noncompetitive
Location: inside or outside

How to Play

Divide the children into two uneven groups (for six children, divide into a group of four and a group of two; for seven children divide into a group of three and a group of four, and so on). The larger of the two groups sits down, and each person shuts his or her eyes. The other children stand next to one another in a line. When an adult says, "Go," one by one the children standing creep up to a player and tap him or her on the head and then return to line. When all the standing players have tapped sitting players, the adult tells the sitting players to open their eyes. Now all the sitting players who were tapped are asked to stand up. One by one they try to guess who tapped them. If a player guesses correctly, he or she changes places with that person. If a player guesses incorrectly, he or she sits down and waits to play the next round.

112

Simon Says

Age Level: 3 and up
Number of Players: 2 or more
What Is Needed: nothing
Type of Game: competitive or noncompetitive
Location: inside or outside

How to Play

An adult or the birthday child is Simon at first. Simon faces the rest of the players, who stand where they can see Simon well. Simon gives commands for the children to follow, such as "Simon says, 'Clap your hands,'" or "Simon says, 'Kick your feet.'" The children are to obey only those commands that begin with the words "Simon says." If the command does not begin with these words (for example, "Stamp your feet"), the players should ignore it.

Competitive Version

Any player who obeys a command not preceded by "Simon says" is out. Speed up the game as the children get good at it. The last player left wins.

Noncompetitive Version

Enjoy a good laugh with the child who obeys a wrong command, but do not send this child out of the game. Keep on playing until interest wanes.

Singing games for very young children

Age Level: 2 and up
Number of Players: 2 or more
What You Need: nothing
Type of Game: noncompetitive
Location: inside or outside

Head, Shoulders, Knees, and Toes

Head, shoulders, knees, and toes,
Knees and toes;
Head, shoulders, knees, and toes,
Knees and toes-s and—
Eyes and ears
And mouth and nose,
Head, shoulders, knees, and toes,
Knees and toes.

Sing to the tune of "There Is a Tavern in the Town." As you name each part of the body, put your hand on the part mentioned. The result is good exercise! Make up additional verses by naming other parts of the body: heels and nose, neck and waist, for example.

I'm a Little Teapot

I'm a little teapot,
Short and stout;
Here is my handle,   *(Put arm on hip.)*
Here is my spout.   *(Bend other arm up.)*
When I'm ready,
Then I shout,
Tip me over   *(Bend to the side.)*
And pour me out.

Ring-a-Ring-a-Roses

Ring-a-ring-a-roses
A pocket full of posies
A-tishoo, a-tishoo
We all fall down.

Join hands and walk around in a circle, falling down at the end.

If You're Happy and You Know It

If you're happy and you know it,
Clap your hands. *(Clap, clap.)*
If you're happy and you know it,
Clap your hands. *(Clap, clap.)*
If you're happy and you know it,
Then your face will surely show it,
If you're happy and you know it,
Clap your hands. *(Clap, clap)*

If you don't know the tune of this
song, you can chant it. The results
will still be effective. Make up other
verses with other actions: shake your
head, touch your nose, jump up and
down, kick your feet, and so on.

Mulberry Bush

Here we go round the mulberry
  bush,
The mulberry bush, the mulberry
  bush.
Here we go round the mulberry
  bush,
So early in the morning.

This is the way we wash our clothes,
Wash our clothes, wash our clothes.
This is the way we wash our clothes,
So early Monday morning.

This is the way we iron our
  clothes, *(etc.)*
So early Tuesday morning.

This is the way we scrub our floor,
  (etc.)
So early Wednesday morning.

This is the way we mend our
  clothes, *(etc.)*
So early Thursday morning.

This is the way we sweep our
  house, *(etc.)*
So early Friday morning.

This is the way we bake our
  bread, *(etc.)*
So early Saturday morning.

This is the way we go to sleep in bed,
  (etc.)
So early Sunday morning.

*Hold hands and skip around in a
circle during the chorus. During the
verses, stop and act out the words of
the song.*

115

Snatch the Flag

Age Level: 5 and up
Number of Players: 5 or more
What Is Needed: a handkerchief or piece of cloth for each player
Type of Game: competitive
Location: outside

How to Play

Everybody puts a handkerchief in a back pocket or back waistband. Part of the handkerchief should be hanging out. The object is for each person to get other players' "flags" without losing his or her own. The rules: no tackling and tripping; anyone who loses a flag must go and sit on the sidelines. The winner is the last person to have a flag.

Sneaky Pete

Age Level: 4 and up
Number of Players: 4 or more
What Is Needed: a chair, something to put under it (a
   pillow, stuffed animal, plastic cup, or toy car), a
   blindfold
Type of Game: noncompetitive
Location: inside or outside

How to Play

Everyone except It (the birthday child at first) lines up,
one behind the other. It sits, blindfolded, on a chair
about six feet away from the first child in line. An object (let's say a stuffed bear) is placed under the chair.
The first person in line crawls or tiptoes toward the
chair and tries to snatch the bear under the chair and
bring it back to the line. It waves his or her hands and
feet and tries to hear or feel this player coming. If It
tags the player, the other player becomes It. If the player gets the bear and goes back to the line without being
tagged, It remains on the chair. The bear is returned
and the next player in line tries to get it.

Spud

Age Level: 7 and up
Number of Players: 3 or more
What Is Needed: a football, beach ball, or other ball that size
Type of Game: noncompetitive
Location: outside

How to Play

The players number off and remember their numbers. It (the birthday child at first) throws the ball up into the air, calling a number at the same time. The player whose number has been called tries to catch the ball. If he or she doesn't catch it, the birthday child throws again and calls out a different number. If the player does catch the ball, he or she can take up to three big steps and throw the ball at any other player. If someone is hit, that player gets an *S*. The birthday child can take up to three more steps and throw the ball at another player. The players dance around the birthday child, trying to avoid being hit but tempting the birthday child to try for them. The birthday child continues to try to hit them, and as they are hit, they get the letters *S*, *P*, *U*, and *D*. The first to spell Spud becomes the next It.

SIX!

118

Stone

Age Level: 5 and up
Number of Players: 4 or more
What Is Needed: nothing
Type of Game: competitive or noncompetitive
Location: outside

How to Play

Establish a start line and a finish line. All the players line up at the start line except the Stone, who can be the birthday child at first. The Stone crouches between the start and finish lines. When an adult says, "Go," the players at the start line tiptoe toward the finish line. At any point the adult can yell, "The Stone is alive! Run!"

At this point everyone runs to the finish line or back to the start line. If a player is tagged by the Stone before reaching either line, this player becomes a Stone too. Players who reach the finish line rest and watch the rest of the game.

Competitive Version

The last player to be made a Stone wins.

Noncompetitive Version

The last player to be made a Stone becomes the one to yell "The Stone is alive!" in the next round.

Treasure Hunt

Age Level: 5 and up

Number of Players: 2 or more

What Is Needed: clues in envelopes, hidden ahead of time (picture clues for nonreaders, printed clues for readers)

Type of Game: competitive or noncompetitive

Location: inside or outside

How to Play

Start by telling the birthday child to look in a certain place for a clue inside an envelope. The envelope has his or her name on it. When found, it is opened by the birthday child. The clue directs all the children to another spot, where another envelope is found with another child's name on it. That child opens it. This clue directs everyone to another spot, and so on. The last clue directs the children to the treasure: a box of goodies that the birthday child opens and shares with all. Suggested treasures are lollipops, raisins, gifts, paperback books, treat bags, or bags of potato crisps.

Competitive Version

Divide the children into two teams with different clues in different spots but leading to the same treasure. The team that finds it first wins, but there are enough goodies inside to share with everyone.

THE OUTSIDE OF THE GARAGE! LET'S GO!

GO TO THE OUTSIDE OF THE GARAGE

Treat Bag* Game

Age Level: 3 and up
Number of Players: 2 or more
What Is Needed: a treat bag for each child, radio or
    record or tape player for music
Type of Game: noncompetitive
Location: inside or outside

How to Play

Ask the children to sit in a circle. Give the birthday
child a treat bag to start passing when the music starts.
The children keep passing the treat bag until the music
stops. Whoever has it then keeps the bag and leaves the
circle. Continue until all the children have a treat bag.
This is a good game, especially for four-to-six-year-olds,
to play at the end of a party, since treat bags are often
handed out then. The children can even put on their
coats beforehand.

*A treat bag is a lunch bag or other bag filled with goodies, such as a banana, a
pencil, a box of raisins, a bar of chocolate, a lollipop, and a handful of crisps. Treat
bags are often passed out at the end of a party so the children have something to
take home.

Twenty Questions

Age Level: 6 and up
Number of Players: 3 or more
What Is Needed: a pad and a pencil to count the questions
Type of Game: noncompetitive
Location: inside or outside

How to Play

Ask the children to sit in a circle. It (the birthday child at first) thinks of something with which everyone at the party is familiar. The children take turns, going around the circle, starting with the child on the birthday child's right, asking questions in order to guess what the thing is. Each question must be a yes-or-no question; that is, it must be asked in such a way as to be answered by the word *yes* or *no*. For example, "Is it alive?" "Is it a person?" "Is it a person in this room?" "Is it a girl?" An adult counts the questions on the pad and tells how many have been used up. If by twenty no one has guessed correctly, It tells the answer. Then the next person to It's left in the circle becomes the next It. If someone guesses the answer, this person becomes the next It.

Who Am I?

Age Level: 8 and up
Number of Players: 2 or more
What Is Needed: cards with names of famous people or characters on them, tape
Type of Game: competitive or noncompetitive
Location: inside or outside

How to Play

As each guest arrives, tape a card with a famous name on it to each person's back, but don't tell what the card says. Each guest has to figure out who he or she is by asking others at the party yes-or-no questions about the person. For example, "Am I a man?" "Am I under the age of 15?" "Am I in sports?" "Do I have blond hair?"

Competitive Version

The first person to figure out who he or she is wins. The last person gets a booby prize.

Noncompetitive Version

Play until everyone finds out who he or she is. Perhaps give everyone something (an armband, a gold star on the forehead) at the moment of discovery.

This is often a good game to play at the beginning of a party, especially if guests don't know each other. It helps everyone get acquainted.

Chapter 4

Special Projects

Let's say you would like to do something special at your party, something a little different, something to remember. Fine. Pick one thing. You don't need to go overboard. Remember: it is in small, subtle, everyday ways that we show our children we really care. Big, flashy, extra-special birthday party treats don't do that job and aren't really necessary, but . . . they can be fun.

When I was five, I went to a birthday party I'll never forget. It was in a tiny house, and when I entered, I found, much to my amazement, that the tiny living room was covered in a web of string. I was handed the end of one string and told to wind it up until I found my prize. Other children were already in the process of unwinding their strands in the huge, intricate, criss-crossing web. I remember nothing else from the party.

One special thing, such as the spider web, is enough. In this chapter you'll find other ideas.

Aprons

Make simple cooking aprons for each child to wear at cooking parties and to take home as favours. With a laundry-marking pen, write the children's names on their aprons ahead of time.

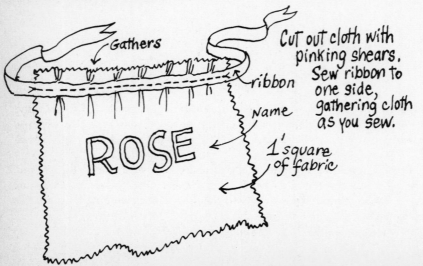

Gathers

ribbon

Name

ROSE

1' square of fabric

Cut out cloth with pinking shears. Sew ribbon to one side, gathering cloth as you sew.

ROSE

Cakes

Make a memorable cake. It may be the biggest cake in the world or the cake with the most candles. It may be a cake the birthday child decorates with sweets or hundreds and thousands. Or it may be that you give each child a cupcake to decorate with frosting and chocolate drops set on the table. Afterward, you might have a contest and give awards of distinction to the children for their cupcakes: the funniest, the sloppiest, the neatest, the prettiest, the most decorated, the wildest, the most delicious-looking, and so on.

Crayon bags

Make wallet-style bags with pockets to hold a small box of crayons and a small pad of paper. Use coloured felt and sew them on a sewing machine. Write each child's name on a bag. Give out the bags as special favours, perhaps in time for them to use the bags for an art activity during the party.

CUT →

FOLD UP AND SEW ↓

FOLD FLAP DOWN ↑

FILL WITH CRAYONS

SADIE

Beanbags

Make beanbags at your party. Sew the three sides of the bags ahead of time. Put a big bowl of assorted beans (kidney, pinto, lentils) on the table where everyone can reach it, and let the children fill their bags. Staple the open ends closed, or let the children sew their bags closed. Play Bull's-Eye Toss with the beanbags. Each child takes home as a party favour the beanbag he or she made. Make sure the children are old enough to know *not* to eat the dried beans.

Balloons

Rent a machine that blows up helium balloons (look in the Yellow Pages). Cover the ceiling with balloons with long strings hanging from them. Each child gets a balloon, or a bouquet of them, to take home. Write each child's name on a balloon with a laundry-marking pen. For more ideas, see Bubbles and Balloons Party. Avoid using balloons for very young children. They can put pieces of popped balloons in their mouths and choke on them.

Piñatas

Make a piñata by putting several strong grocery bags inside one another. Fill with wrapped sweets, small bags of peanuts, small boxes of raisins, and bags of crisps. Tie tightly and knot securely. Decorate either at the party or ahead of time, using crayons, markers, and strips of paper pasted on the bag. Often a piñata is made to look like an animal face, such as a lion, a monster, or a dog with floppy ears. At the party, hang the piñata from a tree or from the ceiling. Let the children take turns, blindfolded, trying to hit the piñata with a broom or plastic cricket bat. (Make sure the other children stand back.) Eventually, the piñata will break and the candy will fall out for everyone to share.

Make a clubhouse or a quilt together

At the party make a clubhouse or a quilt for the birthday child. Precut the wood for the clubhouse and have things ready so the children can help put the house together. Don't have too many guests. Three or four is fine. They should be seven or older. Another grownup would be helpful. To make a quilt together, give each child a 12-by-12-inch square of pastel cotton cloth. Have each of them draw a self-portrait on the square with permanent markers and sign his or her name and the date. Later, as the children play, have a grownup at the party sew the squares together on a sewing machine so that everyone can see what the quilt will look like. Later, add pre-quilted fabric for the reverse side and finish the edges with blanket binding.

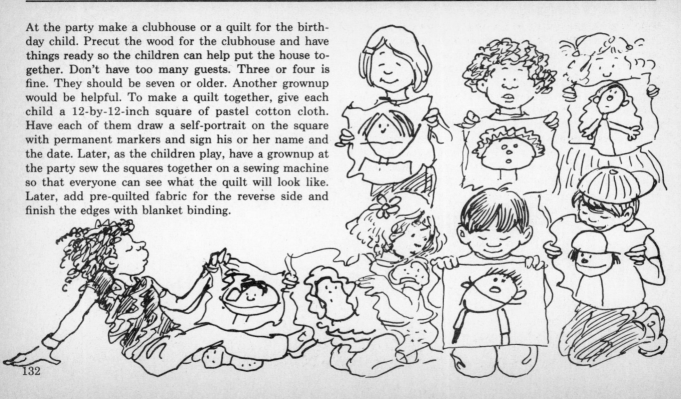

Special guests

Invite someone special to the party, such as Santa Claus, a clown, a magician, a fortune-teller, a storyteller from the library, or a naturalist from a local zoo or nature centre. The naturalist may bring wild animals to show the children. The fortune-teller may be a friend in disguise. Help her write the fortunes ahead of time. Part of the fortune might be a forfeit: "In order to hear your fortune, you must do five somersaults." If you do invite a special guest to the party, make sure the guest doesn't steal the show away from the birthday child. Don't let the person go on too long. If anyone is chosen as a helper, it should be the birthday child.

133

Puppets

Make puppets out of old socks, paper bags, or wooden spoons. Attach ribbons, lace, yarn, and fabric scraps with tape or glue. Draw faces. Then put on a puppet show for the parents when they come at the end of the party.

Surprise Balls

Before the party, make Surprise Balls for each child. Children love them. To make them: wind a strip of crepe paper around and around a small toy (such as a plastic dinosaur or a tiny doll). Keep winding, placing other small toys and wrapped sweets at intervals under the crepe paper. Each ball should contain about ten to twenty things and be about 4 or 5 inches across. Hide the Surprise Balls and have a Surprise Balls Hunt so each child can find and unwrap one. This is a good activity to end a party, and all of the items you might put in a Treat Bag, you can put in a Surprise Ball.

Necklaces and Jewellery

Make snack necklaces by stringing together raisins and dried fruit, miniature marshmallows, and Lifesavers. Make real necklaces out of beads, baked clay, macaroni, or even marbles. To make marble necklaces, bake glass marbles on a baking sheet in a 500° (Gas mark 9) oven for an hour. Put them immediately into a bowl of ice-cold water. They will crack only on the inside to make shimmering jewels. Attach jewellery loops with glue and then string. To make rings, thread pipe cleaners through buttons and then shape the pipe cleaner into a ring shape that fits you. The children can help make jewellery at the party.

PIPE CLEANER →

← BUTTON

Junk sculptures

Save toilet-paper rolls, paper-towel rolls, orange-juice cans, margarine tubs, colourful catalogues, string, bottle tops, and so on. Keep them in a big box somewhere. At the party bring the box out, provide glue or paste, twist ties, and more string, and see what the children can make. Have a contest. Give ribbons or stickers for the most interesting, the smallest, the prettiest, the funniest, the best animal, the best monster, and so on.

Kites

Make paper-bag kites at the party. Give each child a strong paper bag to decorate with markers. Fold the open edge of the bag back about 1½ inches. Tape a 5-inch piece of kite string to each corner of the open end. Join the four strings together and knot them. Add a long piece of string (about 5 or 6 feet) to the place where you knotted the others. To fly the kite, hold the string and run. The bag should fly in the air.

Squirt-Gun Special

If it is warm out, give the children squirt guns and a tub of water and let them go at it outside. Give out bubble-blowing equipment too and see if the children can shoot the bubbles they make. If possible, take movies of this party.

Chapter 5

Food

On the following pages are food suggestions for a child's birthday party. Some of the recipes are very easy to follow and can be done at the last minute; others, such as making homemade ice cream, are more time-consuming. Often the more time-consuming projects are fun for children to help with, but you must allow enough time for them to go at their own pace. You might consider having the birthday child help before the party, or you might consider making the food project part of the party itself. (For example, see Make-Your-Own Cupcake Party, pp. 48–9.)

It is not necessary to serve a meal at a birthday party unless, of course, you plan the party for a mealtime hour. Some parents like to serve meals for the very practical reason that meals keep children seated and occupied for a longer amount of time than just cake and ice cream do. If you serve a meal, keep it simple, and make most of your preparations ahead of time so you don't have to cook during the party. If you want to grill hamburgers during the party, have another grownup do it—and for safety reasons, keep the children away from the cooking area.

If you object to the high amount of sugar in traditional birthday-party sweets, consider serving the Bunny Rabbit Salad, the Help-Yourself Tray of Snacks, Fruit Juice Popsicles, or the Watermelon Surprise, all described in this chapter. Also several of the Party Punch recipes are sugar-free.

3 Easy cakes (yellow, chocolate, & spice)

8 oz caster sugar
4 oz butter
2 eggs
4 fl. oz milk
8 oz plain flour
½ teaspoon milk
2¼ teaspoons baking powder
1 teaspoon vanilla

1. Beat the sugar and butter until they are well mixed.

2. Add the rest of the ingredients. Beat for 2–3 minutes.

3. Bake in a greased 9-by-13-inch tin, or in two greased 8-inch sandwich tins at 350° (Gas mark 4) for 30–35 minutes, or in paper baking cups (filled about ½ full) set in tartlet tins at 350° (Gas mark 4) for 20–25 minutes, or until done.

4. Cook and ice with the frosting of your choice.

Variations

For a CHOCOLATE CAKE, omit 4 tablespoons flour and add 4 tablespoons baking cocoa. For a SPICE CAKE, add 1 teaspoon cinnamon and ½ teaspoon cloves.

Special cakes and cupcakes

Rainbow Cake

Make each layer of cake a different colour. Divide the batter into smaller bowls and tint each batch with food colouring.

Picture Cake

Bake a flat cake in a 9-by-13-inch cake tin. Frost it with one colour and let the frosting harden. Ask your child what he or she wants to show on the cake. Draw the picture on the frosting with a toothpick, then fill it in with different shades of icing. Your child can help.

Design Cake

Bake a flat cake in a 9-by-13-inch tin. Frost it, and while the frosting is still soft, let your child make a design on the cake with gumdrops, miniature marshmallows, raisins, and/or hundreds and thousands.

Fortune Cupcakes

Write fortunes on small pieces of paper. Roll them up. Put one in the batter of each cupcake before baking. Bake, cool, and frost. Tell the children to watch for them and not to eat them! Don't use this idea with younger children.

Fortune Pancakes

Make some pancakes. Roll a fortune on paper inside. Pinch ends of pancake closed. Fold ends under and let cool. They will hold their shape.

Candle Holders

Place Lifesaver sweets on the cake. In each one put a candle.

Frosting ideas and recipes

Butter Frosting

Blend until creamy 2 oz soft butter or margarine, 8 oz icing sugar, 1 teaspoon vanilla, and a dash of salt. if too thin, add more sugar. If too thick, add water or milk by the dropful.

Chocolate Frosting

Make butter frosting and add 2 oz melted cooking chocolate or 1 oz baking cocoa.

Cream Cheese Frosting

Beat 3 oz cream cheese with 4 oz icing sugar. Add ½ teaspoon vanilla.

Whipped Cream Frosting

Beat 1½ pints double cream until thick. Add 1 teaspoon vanilla and 2½ oz icing sugar and continue beating until peaks stand up in the whipped cream. For chocolate flavour, add some powdered chocolate drink or hot cocoa mix to taste.

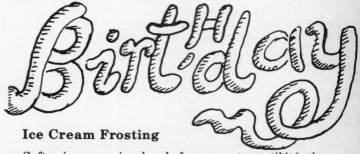

Ice Cream Frosting

Soften ice cream in a bowl of warm water until it is the right consistency to spread. Frost the cake with the ice cream quickly. (This is easiest to do if you have baked the cake in a flat pan.) Freeze it. Before serving, let the cake stand for 10 minutes. Then cut it in squares or slices, and, if you like, pour chocolate sauce over each portion.

Decorator's Icing for Writing on Cakes

Beat together 3 egg whites and a pinch of cream of tartar. Slowly add 1 lb icing sugar. Beat until the icing is stiff enough to hold a line on the counter. Add drops of food colouring to get the colour you desire. Spoon the icing into a small plastic bag. Snip a tiny corner off one of the lower corners. Hold the bag in your hand and squeeze the frosting through the hole to make a line. Practise on greaseproof paper until you can control the line. Then decorate your cake.

No Time? 5 Solutions

1. When you take a cake or cupcakes from the oven, sprinkle with chocolate chips or small peppermints. These toppings will melt and make a sort of icing.

2. Sprinkle slightly cooled cake or cupcakes with grated chocolate, hundreds and thousands, coloured sugar, or icing sugar. These will stick but not melt.

3. Let the children frost their own cupcakes during the party.

4. Don't bother with frosting. Did you ever notice that many children do not like it? It's too sweet and sticky for them. Unfrosted cake and ice cream go well together.

5. Freeze your cake before you frost it. You'll find it easier to work with and faster to frost because the cold temperature helps the icing harden.

Homemade vanilla ice cream (no ice cream maker needed)

You don't need an ice cream maker to make homemade ice cream: the recipe for vanilla ice cream and the recipe for sherbet given on these pages do not require one. But both do have to be prepared ahead of time because they take longer to freeze than ice cream in a maker. If you have an ice cream maker, consider making fresh ice cream during the party. Use the recipes in your instruction book.

6 eggs	1 teaspoon vanilla
8 oz caster sugar	¾ pt double cream
¾ pt milk	

1. Beat the eggs until thick and pale yellow.
2. Add sugar, milk, and vanilla. Mix well.
3. Whip the cream separately and then fold into the egg mixture.
4. Pour into two refrigerator trays and freeze until solid enough to break into pieces.
5. Beat again in a bowl until fluffy but not melted.
6. Pour back into trays and freeze until firm.
7. Before serving, let the ice cream soften a little.

Homemade sherbet & ice cream and sherbet pie

¾ pt mashed fruit   Juice of 2 oranges
   (strawberries, pine- 16 oz caster sugar
   apple, pears, peaches)   ¾ pt single cream
2 mashed bananas
Juice of 2 lemons

1. Beat all ingredients together until they are thoroughly blended.

2. Pour into two refrigerator trays and freeze for 1 hour.

3. Remove the trays from the freezer and stir the mixture in each tray.

4. Freeze 1 hour longer, or until firm.

Ice Cream and Sherbet Pie

Soften vanilla ice cream and any flavour of sherbet. Spread the vanilla ice cream into a flan tin, shaping it into a crust. Fill with sherbet. Freeze. Before serving, soften slightly.

147

Ice cream cake & ice cream cupcakes

Ice cream, any flavour. You can buy several blocks of
different flavours, if you wish.
1 packet of chocolate wafer biscuits.

1. Put the ice cream in the sink to soften for a half
hour.
2. Line a 9-inch spring-form tin with the chocolate
biscuits.
3. Spoon the softened ice cream into the tin quickly.
If you want, make layers of different kinds, pressing
the scoops down to eliminate air spaces. If things
become too messy, put everything in the freezer for a
few minutes to firm up.
4. When you have filled the tin with ice cream, cover
the top with whole biscuits or biscuit crumbs. Cover
with foil and freeze.
5. Before serving, thaw for about 10 minutes or until
the top is soft enough to hold candles.

Ice Cream Cupcakes

Set paper baking cups in a tartlet tin. Place a chocolate
biscuit in each cup. Add a big scoop of softened ice
cream. Top with a biscuit, pressing down slightly, and
freeze until party time. Or bake cupcakes, cool, fill the
rest of the paper baking cup with softened ice cream,
and freeze.

Fruit juice and yogurt lollipops

Fruit juice, any kind or combination of kinds. Use
  your imagination.
Small paper cups
Lollipop sticks.

1. Place the cups in a baking tin.
2. Fill with juice.
3. Stick in lollipop sticks. If you want the stick to
stand up straight in the centre (not necessary), freeze
juice in the cups until slushy, then insert sticks.
4. Freeze until firm.
5. To eat, peel the paper away.

Yogurt Lollipops

Mix plain yogurt and frozen juice concentrate to taste.
Freeze in paper cups with lollipop sticks.

149

Make-your-own ice cream sundaes

Ice cream, various flavours
Sauces (hot fudge, butterscotch, strawberry)
Chopped walnuts
Grated coconut
Hundreds and thousands
Cherries
Whipped cream

Hot Fudge Sauce

In a heavy saucepan melt an 8-oz bar of chocolate, 1 oz butter, and 3 tablespoons milk. Stir and serve. Do not burn.

Butterscotch Sauce

Use butterscotch and follow the procedure for Hot Fudge Sauce.

Strawberry Sauce

Thaw frozen sliced strawberries (the ones that have sugar added).

1. Place the ingredients on the table.
2. Ask the guests to help themselves.

Banana splits

Bananas
Vanilla ice cream
Chocolate ice cream
Strawberry ice cream
Sauces (see Make-Your-Own Ice Cream Sundaes)
Whipped cream
Chopped walnuts
Cherries

1. For each banana split, cut a banana lengthwise and lay both halves side by side on a plate or in a banana-split dish.
2. Place a scoop of vanilla, chocolate, and strawberry ice cream in a row on top of the banana.
3. Add sauce, whipped cream, nuts, and a cherry on top.

Cheesecake (recipe makes 2)

1 lb softened cream
   cheese
5 oz caster sugar
3 eggs
1 pt sour cream

1 oz caster sugar
½ teaspoon vanilla
2 digestive biscuit cases,
   unbaked

1. Add the sugar and eggs to the softened cream cheese and beat well.

2. Pour the mixture into the two biscuit cases, dividing it evenly between them.

3. Bake for 20 minutes at 350° (Gas mark 4). Remove from oven.

4. Beat the sour cream, sugar, and vanilla at high speed for 10 minutes. Pour and spread on the pies.

5. Bake for 10 more minutes at 450° (Gas mark 8).

Note: This cheesecake freezes well.

Popcorn balls

A knob of butter
6 oz molasses
2 oz caster sugar
1½ lb popcorn, lightly salted

1. Melt the butter in a heavy pan.
2. Add the molasses and sugar. Stir until the sugar is dissolved. Boil without stirring to the hard-ball stage (290°).
3. Have the popcorn ready in a large bowl.
4. Slowly pour the syrup over the popcorn, stirring so that every kernel is coated.
5. Butter your hands with soft butter or margarine.
6. Shape the popcorn by hand into balls as soon as it is cool enough to handle. Set the balls on greaseproof paper to cool further and harden.
7. Wrap the cooled popcorn balls individually in greaseproof paper or coloured cellophane. Tie with ribbons.

Pigs-in-blankets & doughboys

Pigs-in-blankets

Follow the instructions on a packet of ready-mix pastry.
Divide the dough into 6 pieces. Flatten each piece and
wrap it around a Frankfurter sausage. Moisten the
edges of the dough and press them together to seal,
leaving the sausage sticking out at each end. To cook,
put on a stick and roast carefully over the barbecue
until cooked. Or, place on an ungreased baking tin and
bake for 15 minutes at 450° (Gas mark 8).

Doughboys

Mix 12 oz ready-mix pastry and ½ pt milk to form a
dough. Wrap the dough around one end of a stick. Use
long thin pieces of dough and wrap them around and
around so that the dough won't fall off the stick. Seal
the edges of the strip together to form one solid cover-
ing. Hold the stick and dough over the coals until the
dough is brown, turning slowly from time to time.
When done, remove the doughboy from the stick with
tongs. Cool slightly. Fill the hole left by the stick with
butter and jam.

Help-yourself tray of snacks

Cheese cubes
Rolled ham slices
Carrot sticks
Celery sticks (can be stuffed
    with cream cheese or
    peanut butter)
Nuts
Bread

Crackers
Rolls
Tomatoes
Strawberries
Dried fruits
Grapes
Apples

1. Select the snacks you want from the list above.
2. Arrange them attractively on plates and platters.
3. Place on a table buffet style.
4. Give the children plates and ask them to serve themselves. Things will go most smoothly if you let the children select whatever they want, with no suggestions from grownups.

Bunny rabbit salad

Pear halves
Slices of bananas cut lengthwise, rubbed or sprinkled
   with lemon juice so they won't turn brown
Lettuce
Raisins
Long, thin carrot sticks

1. Place a leaf of lettuce on each plate.
2. On the lettuce place a pear half, hole down.
3. Add banana ears.
4. Add carrot-stick whiskers.
5. Cut little holes in the pear and insert raisins for
eyes, nose, and mouth.

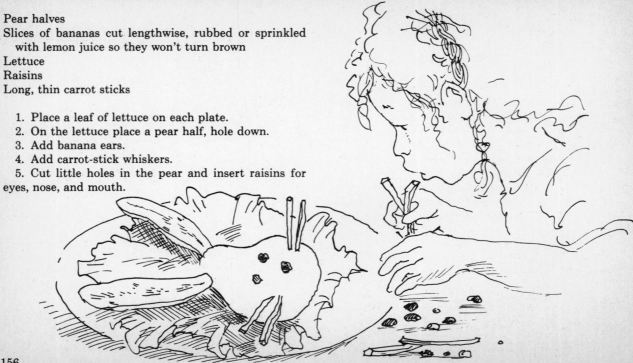

Watermelon surprise

Watermelon
Fruits for fruit cocktail (apples, peaches, pears, bananas, melons, grapes)
Lemon juice

1. Slice off the top third of a watermelon. This will be the lid. Slice ¼ inch off the bottom so the watermelon can stand up securely and serve as a bowl.

2. Scoop out the watermelon, discard the seeds, and cut the watermelon into bite-sized pieces.

3. Cut up the other fruits and mix together gently in a big bowl. Sprinkle lemon juice over the mixture so the fruits do not discolour.

4. Tidy up both sections of the watermelon.

5. Fill the watermelon with the fruit-cocktail mixture.

6. Put the lid on the watermelon.

7. Poke or cut holes in the lid for the birthday candles.

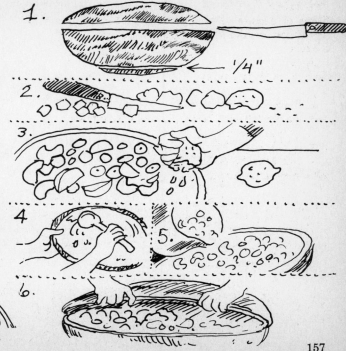

Party punch recipes

Try these recipes out ahead of time to find the proportions you like.

ORANGE JUICE o LEMONADE

GRAPE JUICE and LEMONADE (makes pink lemonade)

SHERBET and GINGER BEER (mix it in a punch bowl and watch it fizz) serve.

APPLE JUICE and 7-UP

BROWN COW Fill up a glass with Coca Cola. Add a scoop of vanilla ice cream

apple juice Lemonade

YOGURT FRUIT JUICE

GINGER BEER FROZEN SLICED STRAW-BERRIES (Thawed)

Lemonade Ginger Beer Water to Taste

CHOCOLATE MILK SHAKE For each person: 1 cup milk 2 scoops chocolate ice cream 2 tablespoons instant cocoa SHAKE IN A BIG JAR AND POUR

Metric conversion tables

1 oz	= 25 g (grammes)	
2 oz	= 50 g	
4 oz	= 100 g	
8 oz	= 225 g	
12 oz	= 350 g	
1 lb	= 450 g	
1½ lb	= 700 g	
2 lb	= 900 g	
2 lb 3 oz	= 1 kg (kilogramme)	

1 tablespoon	= ½ fluid oz	= 15 ml (millilitres)
1 dessertspoon	= ⅔ fluid oz	= 10 ml
1 teaspoon	= ⅕ fluid oz	= 5 ml

¼ pint	= 5 fluid oz	= 150 ml
½ pint	= 10 fluid oz	= 300 ml
¾ pint	= 15 fluid oz	= 450 ml
1 pint	= 20 fluid oz	= 600 ml

10 millitres (ml)	= 1 centilitre (cl)	= ⅖ fluid oz
10 cl (100 ml)	= 1 decilitre (dl)	= 3½ fluid oz
10 dl (1,000 ml)	= 1 litre (l)	= 35 fluid oz

Oven temperatures are different: 350° F (Fahrenheit) is 177° C (Celsius). But you don't have to worry about that. Use the baking temperatures you've always used unless you have a new metric stove.

FOR MEASURING

1 inch	2.54 cm (centimeters)
1 foot	30.48 cm

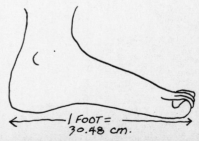

Note: All conversions are approximate. They are rounded off to the nearest convenient measure.

159

Chapter 6

Birthday Record Book

Take a few minutes sometime during the let-down period after the birthday party, or during the week that follows, to jot down a few notes about the party on the pages at the back of this book. At the time this may seem silly, but in years to come, you'll treasure these memories.

I have found that I am usually in such a strange mood, dazed yet wound-up, during my children's parties that months later I can't remember a thing that happened. In the process of writing this book, I went back to the notes I wrote about some of these parties in my children's baby books and found descriptions such as this: "You had white cupcakes with pink frosting, and Mac made you some strawberry Italian ice. Hallie gave you a jersey that said 'Grease' on it, but you wouldn't wear it because it had Olivia Newton-John on it. You're almost grown-up now that you're five. Recently you said to Dad, who was holding you, 'You're comfortabling me, like a blanket.'"

First birthday party

Height _____ Weight_____ Year_____

How the Party Was Celebrated

Food

Games and Activities

Guests

Favourite Gifts

Second birthday party

Height _____ Weight_____ Year_____

How the Party Was Celebrated

Food

Games and Activities

Guests

Favourite Gifts

Third birthday party

Height _____ Weight_____ Year_____

How the Party Was Celebrated

Food

Games and Activities

Guests

Favourite Gifts

Fourth birthday party

Height _____ Weight_____ Year_____

How the Party Was Celebrated

Food

Games and Activities

Guests

Favourite Gifts

Fifth birthday party

Height _____ **Weight** _____ **Year** _____

How the Party Was Celebrated

Food

Games and Activities

Guests

Favourite Gifts

Sixth birthday party

Height _____ Weight_____ Year_____

How the Party Was Celebrated

Food

Games and Activities

Guests

Favourite Gifts

Seventh birthday party

Height _____ Weight_____ Year_____

How the Party Was Celebrated

Food

Games and Activities

Guests

Favourite Gifts

Eighth birthday party

Height _____ Weight_____ Year_____

How the Party Was Celebrated

Food

Games and Activities

Guests

Favourite Gifts

Ninth birthday party

Height _____ Weight_____ Year_____

How the Party Was Celebrated

Food

Games and Activities

Guests

Favourite Gifts

Tenth birthday party

Height _____ Weight _____ Year _____

How the Party Was Celebrated

Food

Games and Activities

Guests

Favourite Gifts

Index

Also published by Unwin Paperbacks

SUPERKIDS

Creative Learning Activities for Children 5-15
by Jean Marzollo
Illustrated by Irene Trivas

Designed for kids who like to *do* things, *Superkids* gives specific ideas for projects and basic instructions for carrying them out. Projects like planting a garden, baking bread, making a home movie, planning a party, building a birdhouse. Older children can use this book on their own, younger ones may need help but as they try the various enjoyable activities, they will gain in skills and learn something about their own talents at the same time.

LEARNING THROUGH PLAY

by Jean Marzollo and Janice Lloyd
Illustrated by Irene Trivas

Play is the natural way children learn and the authors of *Learning Through Play* suggest a wide range of games and activities to amuse small children, that also provide an opportunity to enhance and enlarge upon their skills and achievements. Games for indoors and out, in the car, at the zoo, or on the corner of the kitchen table. Activities that can be easily adapted by playgroups and schools, baby-sitters, relatives and friends. And most of all, activities that are fun.

Supertot *Jean Marzollo, illustrated by
Irene Trivas*   £2.95 ☐
Learning Through Play *Jean Marzollo and Janice
Lloyd, illustrated by Irene Trivas*   £2.95 ☐
Superkids *Jean Marzollo, illustrated by
Irene Trivas*   £2.95 ☐

*All these books are available at your local bookshop or
newsagent, or can be ordered direct by post. Just tick the
titles you want and fill in the form below.*

Name ....

Address ....

....

....

Write to Unwin Cash Sales, PO Box 11, Falmouth,
Cornwall TR10 9EN.
Please enclose remittance to the value of the cover price
plus:
UK: 55p for the first book plus 22p for the second book,
thereafter 14p for each additional book ordered to a
maximum charge of £1.75.
BFPO and EIRE: 55p for the first book plus 22p for the
second book and 14p for the next 7 books and thereafter 8p
per book.
OVERSEAS: £1.00 for the first book plus 25p per copy for
each additional book.
Unwin Paperbacks reserve the right to show new retail
prices on covers, which may differ from those previously
advertised in the text or elsewhere. Postage rates are also
subject to revision.